7.50

THE BASIS FOR THE BUILDING WORK OF GOD

WITNESS LEE

Living Stream Ministry
Anaheim, CA • www.lsm.org

First Edition, October, 2003.

ISBN 0-7363-2294-9

Published by

Living Stream Ministry
2431 W. La Palma Ave., Anaheim, CA 92801 U.S.A.
P. O. Box 2121, Anaheim, CA 92814 U.S.A.

Printed in the United States of America

03   04   05   06   07   08   09   /   9   8   7   6   5   4   3   2   1

CONTENTS

PREFACE

In the summer of 1958 Brother Witness Lee, a servant of the Lord, was sent by God to Europe, America, and Asia to visit the saints and to observe the condition of the churches in these places. Upon returning to Taiwan, he was heavily burdened in his heart due to his sense that there is a tremendous lack of building among the churches today. Subsequently he released ten messages in the eleventh conference for the whole island of Taiwan. These messages have been published in the book *The Building Work of God*. In order to strengthen the revelation contained in these first ten messages, Brother Lee gave another eight messages, entitled "The Basis for the Building Work of God." On the one hand, our brother saw that God's eternal will, His ultimate goal, is to build a house that is the mingling and the mutual dwelling of God and man. On the other hand, he realized that despite the presence of Christianity and of Christians all over the earth, there is the lack of such a house. Although there are people in many places who love the Lord, who zealously pursue the Lord, and who pay attention to spiritual things, it is hard to find one group of Christians who have been built together to become a spiritual house in which God can dwell, a house that satisfies the needs of both God and man. Not only do we not have the reality of the building; we lack even the concept of the building up of the church. Most Christians have as their goal getting saved and going to heaven and are ignorant of the revelation of the building of the church. These eight messages are directed at this situation. On the one hand, they aim to make known God's will and to point out His goal; on the other hand, they aim to correct our mistakes and to inspire us in our pursuit.

Everyone should have a copy of this book; it is one that must be read.

Chang Yu-lan
May 15, 1959
Taipei, Taiwan

CHAPTER ONE

THE RELATIONSHIP
BETWEEN JOHN'S WRITINGS
AND THE BUILDING WORK OF GOD

We will begin by reading a number of passages from the Bible which are all very important. I hope everyone would pay attention in reading them. John 1:1-4 says, "In the beginning was the Word, and the Word was with God, and the Word was God. He was in the beginning with God. All things came into being through Him, and apart from Him not one thing came into being which has come into being. In Him was life, and the life was the light of men." Verse 14 says, "And the Word became flesh and tabernacled among us (and we beheld His glory, glory as of the only Begotten from the Father), full of grace and reality," and verse 18 continues, "No one has ever seen God; the only begotten Son, who is in the bosom of the Father, He has declared Him." Then 2:19-21 says, "Jesus answered and said to them, Destroy this temple, and in three days I will raise it up. Then the Jews said, This temple was built in forty-six years, and You will raise it up in three days? But He spoke of the temple of His body."

Chapter one of John says that the Lord Jesus' becoming flesh was His erecting a tabernacle among men. In chapter two the Lord shows us that His body was a temple. In the Old Testament among the Israelites, first there was a tabernacle and later there was a temple. The tabernacle and the temple were really the same thing in two different time periods. These two passages show us that the Lord Jesus became a man as the tabernacle and the temple.

John 2:22 says, "When therefore He was raised from the dead, His disciples remembered that He had said this, and they believed the Scripture and the word which Jesus had spoken." Here we see that the body of the Lord Jesus is a temple not only due to His incarnation but also to His resurrection. On the one hand, His flesh was a tabernacle; on the other hand, it was a temple. When the Jews sought to kill Him, the Lord indicated that they were seeking to destroy the temple. However, the Lord also said that in three days He would raise up the temple which the Jews would destroy. This meant that the Jews would kill Him and He would be raised in three days (vv. 18-22).

Verse 3 of chapter fourteen says, "Where I am you also may be," and verse 10 says, "I am in the Father." Therefore, we need to note that the word *where* repeatedly mentioned in John 14 is a matter not of a place but of a person. Here it is concerned not with where the Lord Jesus is but in whom He is. Where is the Lord Jesus? He is in the Father.

Verse 11 says, "Believe Me that I am in the Father and the Father is in Me." Then verse 19 says, "Yet a little while and the world beholds Me no longer, but you behold Me; because I live, you also shall live." These verses show us that after the Lord Jesus resurrected, He regenerated us, enabling us to live just as He lives. "Yet a little while and the world beholds Me no longer, but you behold Me." The "little while" here is only three days. Three days after His crucifixion, the Lord Jesus resurrected and entered into the disciples as the Spirit. Because of this, the world beheld the Lord no longer, but the disciples beheld Him.

Verse 20 says, "In that day you will know that I am in My Father, and you in Me, and I in you." The phrase *that day* refers to the day mentioned in verse 19, in which the world would no longer behold the Lord, but the disciples would behold Him, and in which the disciples would live because He would live.

Verse 4 of chapter fifteen says, "Abide in Me and I in you." In the Greek language, there are at least two words with the general sense of "to reside." One of them means to make home, as in Ephesians 3:17, which says, "That Christ may make His home in your hearts through faith." The word here is a very emphatic word and is best translated as *make home*. The other word, like the one in John 15, means to stay and not depart. Verse 5 says, "I am the vine; you are the branches. He who abides in Me and I in him...."

Then 17:20 says, "And I do not ask concerning these only, but concerning those also who believe into Me through their word." In verse 20, *these* refers to the disciples who were with the Lord Jesus on the night of His betrayal. However, *those* refers to those who believe into the Lord through their word. It is much more inclusive, including all who would believe in the Lord over the next two thousand years through the gospel preached by the apostles. Therefore, here the Lord is praying for all those who belong to Him.

Verse 21 says, "That they all may be one; even as You, Father, are in Me and I in You, that they also may be in Us; that the world may believe that You have sent Me." How were the disciples one? They were one as the Triune God is one. This oneness causes the world to believe that God has sent the Lord. The most powerful way to preach the gospel so that people may believe that Jesus is the Christ of God is the testimony lived out from this oneness. When we who are saved are one in the Triune God, it is easy for the world to believe that the Lord Jesus is the Christ sent by God.

Verses 22 and 23 say, "And the glory which You have given Me I have given to them, that they may be one, even as We are one; I in them, and You in Me, that they may be perfected into one, that the world may know that You have sent Me and have loved them even as You have loved Me." Glory is too great a subject. We cannot explain it in a few sentences. The Lord says that He is able to make us one because He has given to us the glory which the Father has given Him. Here the Lord also mentions love. This love is not the love we commonly speak of. Many suppose that the Lord's giving us peace, food to eat, and clothes to wear, and His caring for all of our needs is His love for us. Here, however, the emphasis is not on these matters and not even on the love shown by the Lord's dying and shedding His blood for us. Here the focus is on God the Father giving glory to all those who belong to His Son that they may be absolutely one in the Triune God.

Verse 24 says, "Father, concerning that which You have given Me, I desire that they also may be with Me where I am, that they may behold My glory, which You have given Me, for You loved Me before the foundation of the world." I would like to ask you, brothers and sisters, what does *where* refer to? Bible expositors mostly agree that *where* refers to heaven. They say that the Lord meant, "I am in heaven, and concerning that which You have given Me, I desire that they also may be with Me in heaven." This is incorrect. We have already discussed that the word *where* in this chapter is not a matter of a place but of a person. The Lord Himself clearly said that He is in the Father and we are also in the Father. Therefore, the phrase *where I am* means "in the Father." The Lord desired that those given to Him by the Father would be with Him in the Father, and once the disciples were in the Father, they could see the glory the Father has given to the Lord. They did not have to wait to go up to heaven one day to see the glory. From the day of the Lord's resurrection, Peter saw the glory that God had given to the Lord because Peter was in the Father with the Lord. He could say, "The Lord in whom I believe is in God the Father; in the same way I am together with Him in God, that is, in the Father. I have known the glory which the Father has given Him."

The Lord's prayer concludes with verse 26: "And I have made Your name known to them and will yet make it known, that the love with which You have loved Me may be in them, and I in them."

Four chapters in the Gospel of John—chapters fourteen through seventeen—are connected. The first three chapters are the last message spoken by the Lord on the earth, and chapter seventeen is a concluding prayer offered by the Lord after He had given the message. If you ask me what the central subject of the Lord's message and concluding prayer is, I would tell you that the central subject is "in." These four chapters talk about "in." Here the Lord is telling the disciples, "I am in the Father, but you who believe Me are not yet in the Father, because you are not in Me and I have not yet come into you. Therefore I am going to do something; I am going to open a way for you, prepare a place for you, that I may bring you into the Father just as I am in the Father. In that day where I am you also may be. I am in the Father, and you also will be in the Father. In that day you will be regenerated, and My resurrection life will be in you that you may live. Therefore, in that day, as I live, you also shall live. Also in that day you will know that I am in My Father, and you in Me, and I in you. This is like a vine and its branches abiding mutually— you abiding in Me and I in you."

After the Lord finished this message, He offered a concluding prayer. The center of this prayer was His asking God concerning those who belong to Him that they may be one in the Triune God just as the Triune God is mutually one. This is the central meaning of these four chapters in the Gospel of John.

1 John 4:13 says, "In this we know that we abide in Him and He in us, that He has given to us of His Spirit." Verses 11 and 12 of chapter five say, "And this is the testimony, that God gave to us eternal life and this life is in His Son. He who has the Son has the life; he who does not have the Son of God does not have the life." Verse 20 says, "And we know that the Son of God has come and has given us an understanding that we might know Him who is true; and we are in Him who is true, in His Son Jesus Christ. This is the true God and eternal life." In the whole universe everything is false; there is only One who is true. Besides Him, everything else is empty and false. At this time John could say, "We are in Him." In John 14 when the Lord Jesus spoke, none of the disciples could say that he was in Him who is true, because at that time they were outside of God; they had not entered into God. However, when John wrote this Epistle, the Lord had already resurrected and ascended, and the Holy Spirit had descended at Pentecost, so John could say, "We are in Him who is true,...the true God." This fulfills the word of the Lord when He seemed to say, "Where I am, you also may be. I am in the Father, and I will also bring you into the Father so that you and I may be in Him together." That is why John could say, "And we are in Him who is true, in His Son Jesus Christ. This is the true God and eternal life."

There is a dispute in Bible translation concerning the word

this in verse 20. Some are in favor of translating it as *this,* while others are in favor of translating it as *He*: "He is the true God and eternal life." It would be very simple to translate it as *He,* referring simply to God's Son Jesus Christ in the previous sentence. However, if we translate it as *this,* then the scope becomes much broader. It then refers not only to the Lord but also includes all the things mentioned in the preceding passage as well. What are these things? They are that we might know Him who is true and that we are in Him who is true, in His Son Jesus Christ. This knowing, this being in the Lord, is the true God and eternal life.

Each of these two translations has its merit, for the truths in the Bible are not at all simple. Here the Bible is not merely telling us that the Lord Jesus is the true God and eternal life. Even more, it is telling us that all the things mentioned previously are included in the Lord Jesus, and this is the true God; this is eternal life. Of course, this is a mysterious word, which we will come to understand only gradually.

We have read John's Gospel and also John's Epistles. We all know that John did not write only these two categories of books; he also wrote a book of prophecy, which is Revelation. John wrote three categories of writings: a Gospel, three Epistles, and a prophecy. We have read from two categories; now let us read from the third category.

Revelation 21:2-3 says, "And I saw the holy city, New Jerusalem, coming down out of heaven from God, prepared as a bride adorned for her husband. And I heard a loud voice out of the throne, saying, Behold, the tabernacle of God is with men, and He will tabernacle with them, and they will be His peoples, and God Himself will be with them and be their God." Here the tabernacle is mentioned again. *Tabernacle* has the same root as the word *tabernacled* in John 1:14. Here it is a noun, while in John 1:14 it is a verb. The city of New Jerusalem is the tabernacle of God with men. Revelation 21:3 also says that God will tabernacle with men. In other words, in Greek, the word *tabernacle* is mentioned twice in this verse. It is used as a noun the first time, referring to the tabernacle as an entity, and it is used as a verb the second time, referring to the setting up of the tabernacle.

Verse 22 says, "And I saw no temple in it, for the Lord God the Almighty and the Lamb are its temple." Why is there no temple in the city? It is because the city is the tabernacle. We all know that the tabernacle and the temple are one thing. The tabernacle is the precursor of the temple. Now since this city is the tabernacle, and in this sense it is also the temple, it cannot have another temple within it. There was a temple in the city of the old Jerusalem, but the New Jerusalem is itself a temple. If we say there is a temple, then the temple is God Himself. Verse 22 is a marvelous utterance.

THERE BEING A SPECIAL RELATIONSHIP BETWEEN JOHN'S WRITINGS AND THE BUILDING WORK OF GOD

Verses 1 and 2 of chapter 22 say, "And he showed me a river of water of life, bright as crystal, proceeding out of the throne of God and of the Lamb in the middle of its street. And on this side and on that side of the river was the tree of life."

In this conference every evening we will focus on the building of God. In the meetings in the mornings we will give additional words concerning the building of God by reading some portions of the Scriptures.

We have just read some portions from John's Gospel, John's Epistles, and John's prophecy. In these few days we hope to see the building of God in the universe through John's writings. Why are we seeing it from John's writings? It is first because the ultimate manifestation of God's building is revealed to us in the book of Revelation written by John. The manifestation of the New Jerusalem is the completion of God's building in the universe throughout the ages. This is shown to us by John. Hence, if we want to know God's building, we have to read John's writings.

Second, we have said repeatedly that God's work of building in the universe is to have a dwelling place in which He Himself, and also all who belong to God, may dwell. Therefore, God's work of building is to gain a place of dwelling. In the books written by the other apostles, we rarely see statements telling us that God abides in man and man abides in God. In John's writings, however, we can easily find this kind of expression. John clearly and repeatedly speaks of God abiding in man and man abiding in God. This abiding has a very close relationship with God's building. If we would know God's building in the universe, we need to understand the matter of the mutual abiding of God and man. We must understand how God dwells in man and how man dwells in God. For this reason we need to look at John's writings.

Third, from Genesis to Revelation we see that after creation the second step of God's work is His building. The center of the matter of building lies in life. In the garden of Eden God had created everything, but there was no building. Therefore, God shows us that after He created man, He placed him in the center of the garden of Eden, in front of the tree of life. Anyone can realize that God's intention was to have the man He created eat of the fruit of the tree of life that the life of this fruit would enter into man and be mingled with man as one. This mingling is God's building. At the end of Revelation, when the building of God is consummated, there will still be the tree of life in the New Jerusalem. This tells us that there is a definite relationship between the building of God and life. God's building in the universe is altogether completed by His coming into man as life. As food He wants to be received into man, be digested in man, and be mingled with man as one. This mingling is the building. God wants to build Himself into man and also to build man into Himself.

This is like a house built with reinforced concrete, which is built by mingling steel bars with a mixture of cement and gravel. It is the same with God's building in the universe. God wants to be mingled and beaten together with man. How does God mingle Himself with man? He does this by coming to be man's life in the way of food. He wants to come into man as man's food and to be dissolved and digested in man to become man's life.

The illustration of food that the Bible uses to refer to the mingling of God and man is very fitting, since nothing mingles with man as thoroughly as food. After food is eaten and digested by man, it becomes his blood, his bone, and his flesh, completely mingled with him as one. Please do not be offended when I say that we human beings are the result of the mingling of chicken, duck, fish, pork, and beef. Do not assume that you are only human. Consider how much fish, chicken, pork, and beef has been digested in you for you to be built up. When a person is born, his height is at most a little more than a foot, and he weighs seven or eight pounds. However, he later grows to be five or six feet tall and weighs well over a hundred pounds. Why does he grow taller and bigger? It is because of his inward mingling with a good amount of chicken, duck, fish, pork, beef, wheat, and rice.

This is a very good illustration to help us to understand how God comes into us and mingles Himself with us to complete His building. As food, God comes into us to be our bread and our life. In this way God continuously mingles Himself with man to the point that a building comes forth. This building is the New Jerusalem.

Therefore, it is hard to say what exactly the city of New Jerusalem is. There is a great dispute about this among Bible expositors today. Some say that the New Jerusalem is a physical place, while others say that it is just a symbol. However, we need to see this one thing: God is in this city, and the redeemed people are also in this city. In this city, God and the Lamb are the temple, and the redeemed ones throughout the ages are the foundations and the gates. Therefore, this city is the issue of the mingling and building of God with the redeemed ones. This is God's mysterious building in the universe, and it is accomplished by God becoming man's life and mingling Himself with man. Consequently, in this city there will still be the tree of life.

Please remember, the writings of John specifically cover this line. For example, the Gospel of John focuses on God's entering into man to become man's life. Therefore, when the Gospel of John talks about the Lord Jesus who comes to be man's life, it says that He is the bread of life and that He is the vine. If you connect John 6—where the Lord says that He is the bread of life—with what He says in John 15—that He is the vine tree, you can easily see that He is the tree of life coming to be man's life as food, as portrayed in Genesis 2. The tree of life is a tree, and its fruit is man's food. This is exactly what John tells us—that this God who comes to be man's life is the bread of life and He is also a vine tree. For this reason, in order to understand the building of God, we need to read the books written by John.

I will repeat again. First, John particularly shows us that the ultimate manifestation of God's building is the New Jerusalem. Second, God's work of building is to obtain a dwelling place in which both God and man may dwell. In the entire Bible, no one speaks more clearly than John concerning God abiding in man and man abiding in God. Third, God's building is completed by God coming into man to be man's life and by mingling Himself with man, which is precisely John's ministry. These are the three reasons that we must read John's writings.

Due to the limited time, in these messages we cannot read John's writings chapter by chapter and verse by verse. Besides, reading in such a way may not make you clear. If instead we bring out and touch all the main points, you may have a better understanding. Therefore, I beg all the brothers and sisters to read through the Gospel of John and 1 John beforehand. I do not think this is a difficult task.

SOME CHARACTERISTICS OF THE GOSPEL OF JOHN

As we read the Gospel of John, I would like for us to pay attention to several characteristics. This will help us to recognize the main points.

First, in John, time begins with "in the beginning." All those who read the Bible know that the word *beginning* refers to eternity. Since there is no time in eternity, there is no element of time in John. Please make certain to not read time into the Gospel of John. John shows us how the God in eternity came into us to be eternal life. As the Word in eternity past, He was without beginning or end, without the element of time. Even though He came into time and was restricted by time, He imparted to man the eternal life, a life that is beyond time. In this eternal life, there is no element of time.

I would like to insert a word about reading the Bible. Many brothers and sisters assume that since Genesis is the first book in the Bible, narrating from the very beginning, its account is the earliest. However, I would like to tell you that the account in the Gospel of John is even earlier. Why? It is because John begins from eternity past, from an eternity without beginning. The beginning in Genesis has a starting point, which is the time of God's creation. In other words, Genesis starts at the beginning of time, while John starts before time began, in eternity past.

In addition, Genesis begins with God's creation, but John begins with God. Genesis says, "In the beginning God created the heavens and the earth" (1:1). John says, "In the beginning was the Word,...the Word was God" (1:1). It is after he speaks of the God who was in the beginning that he goes on to speak of all things coming into being through Him. Therefore, Genesis begins at John 1:3, with the clause, "All things came into being through Him." The first two verses in John 1 are earlier than Genesis; they precede Genesis. These matters are crucial points in Bible reading. We all have to pay special attention to them.

Second, in the Gospel of John there is not the matter of space. John's Gospel is beyond time and space. John's time is eternity past, and John's space is God. In 3:13 there is a sentence spoken by the Lord Himself which proves that there is no element of space in John's Gospel: "And no one has ascended into heaven, but He who descended out of heaven, the Son of Man, who is in heaven." We do not understand this word because we are full of spatial concepts. However, to the Lord there is no element of space. We often say that the Lord Jesus left heaven and came down to earth. Here though, the Lord Jesus said that He left heaven yet is still in heaven. We also often say that the Lord Jesus left the earth and ascended to the heavens, but I believe the Lord Jesus would say, "No, I left the earth, yet I am still on the earth."

I would like to ask you brothers and sisters where in the whole Gospel of John it says that the Lord Jesus descended out of heaven. You may ask, "Did not the Lord Himself say that He descended out of heaven?" True, but the Lord went on to say that He is still in heaven. Likewise, you cannot find the record of the ascension of the Lord Jesus in the Gospel of John. Mark contains a record of the Lord Jesus' ascension, and so does Luke, but neither John nor Matthew contains such a record. Perhaps you will say that out of the four Gospels there are at least two that mention the Lord Jesus' ascension. You may ask, "Do Mark and Luke not talk about the ascension of the Lord Jesus?" However, if you can pick out two books, I can also pick out two books. Can you tell me where Matthew and John mention the Lord's ascension? You can pick out two books that mention the Lord's ascension; I can also pick out two books that do not mention the Lord's ascension. The two books you pick are neither the beginning nor the end. The two books I pick are at the beginning and at the end. Moreover, of the two books you pick, one portrays Him as a Slave while the other portrays Him as a man. Both are relatively light in weight. Of the two books that do not mention His ascension, one speaks of Him as King while the other speaks of Him as God. The one that says He is King not only does not mention His ascension, but it says that He will be with us until the consummation of the age (Matt. 28:20). The beginning of the Gospel of Matthew says that the Lord is Emmanuel, which is translated "God with us" (1:23). Matthew also says that where there are two or three gathered into the name of the Lord, there He is in their midst (18:20). At the end, it says that the Lord will be with us until the consummation of the age. Matthew tells us that the Lord is Emmanuel and that He comes to rule within us as our spiritual King; therefore, He does not leave us but will be with us until the end of this age.

The Gospel of John says that the Lord is the One from the beginning, from eternity past, who came into our midst. He did not come from heaven to earth but from God to man. This is not a matter of place but a matter of persons. He never left the heavens, and He never left the earth. He says, "Abide in Me" (15:4). This is a fact which we can have today. To abide in the Lord we do not need to go to heaven. We do not need to climb a ladder that goes up to heaven to abide in the Lord for a while and after a few days come down. We do not need this because there is no element of space. The Lord says, "Abide in Me and I in you." Today the Lord Jesus lives in us without having to descend from heaven; likewise, we live in the Lord without having to climb a ladder up to heaven.

This kind of speaking may seem to be a joke, but I am using an illustration to show you that the Gospel of John does not have the element of space. The Lord descended, but He was still in the heavens. After He resurrected, He ascended, but He was still on the earth. After the Lord's resurrection, the disciples were inside the house with its doors and windows shut, and the Lord suddenly came into their midst. This was truly wonderful. Through what did He enter? We do not know. He was not merely a Spirit; He also had a body with bone and flesh. Still, the doors and windows were shut, so we do not know how He entered the house. Then after He spoke to the disciples and told them to receive the Holy Spirit, He disappeared again. We do not know where He went. If we say that He went away, we do not see Him opening the door. He reappeared when Peter and the other disciples went fishing in the sea, and we do not know where He went afterward. When we read the Gospel of John, we cannot find verses telling us where He went.

Why is it that the Gospel of John does not say where the Lord went? It is because in the Gospel of John there is no element of space. Today He is everywhere. Even as we meet here this morning, He is here. If there are one thousand people sitting here this morning, strictly speaking there are not only one thousand but one thousand and one, because the Lord Jesus is here as well. He is One who is beyond time, and He is also One who is beyond space. You need to pay attention to these two points when reading the Gospel of John.

Please remember that in His incarnation He came not from heaven to earth but from God to man. In His death and resurrection He went not from earth to heaven but from man to God. The places John mentions are persons, not actual places.

Third, the entire Gospel of John covers the matter of life being in the Lord. The first verse of this book says, "In the beginning was the Word." This is speaking of the beginning, of God Himself. Then verse 3 speaks of creation, and verse 4 says that in Him was life. The whole universe is a story of life, and this life is in Him. When you read Genesis, you first see creation; then you see life. The life signified by the tree of life in Genesis 2 is in Him. Please pay attention to the sequence in John. John begins by saying that in the beginning was God; then it speaks about God's creation, and then it tells us how God came to be man's life because life was in Him. From this point on, the whole Gospel of John talks about the matter of life being in Him. This is what we need to pay attention to.

Fourth, the Gospel of John is divided into two major sections. One section is on coming, and the other is on going. Chapter one to chapter thirteen is on the Lord's incarnation, His coming. Chapter fourteen is a turning point. Chapter fourteen through the end of the book is on the Lord's death and resurrection, His going. However, the Lord's coming and going here do not have the element of time or space. The Lord's incarnation is God coming among men, God coming into man. The purpose of the Lord's death and resurrection is to bring man into God. There is no element of space or place here.

Therefore, chapter fourteen is a great turning point. Chapter one to chapter thirteen talks about His incarnation, about His bringing God among man and into man, and about His enabling man to see God, touch God, and receive God. These are things related to incarnation, which is God coming among man. However, man had not yet entered into God, so beginning from chapter fourteen, this Gospel speaks about His bringing man into God. Before chapter fourteen there was no such word as "Abide in Me"; He could not say such a word. In chapter fourteen He said, "In that day you will know that...you [are] in Me" (v. 20). Without the arrival of "that day," the disciples could not know, because it was not possible to have such an experience. The story after chapter fourteen is a story of "that day."

Therefore, when we read the Gospel of John, we need to pay attention to these points. Chapters one through thirteen talk about the situation and the story of the Lord's incarnation, which brought God among men and into man. Then starting from chapter fourteen we see the way He took to bring man into God. I hope that you brothers and sisters can follow these principles to properly read the Gospel of John. In the next few days we will specifically focus on studying the writings of John. I believe it will cause us to have a better understanding of the building of God. After studying in this way, we will then understand what exactly God's building in the universe is.

CHAPTER TWO

HOW THE LORD BUILDS UP
THE HOUSE OF GOD

Scripture Reading: John 1:4, 14, 18, 51; 2:16-22

THE LORD'S INCARNATION, DEATH,
AND RESURRECTION
BEING FOR THE BUILDING UP OF THE HOUSE OF GOD

I would like to highlight and briefly explain three points from the Scripture reading above. First, John 1 opens by saying that in the beginning was the Word, the Word was God, in Him was life, and one day this Word became flesh and tabernacled among men. These are great words with deep and wide connotations. We need to have a deep understanding of the background of the Old Testament in order to understand the meaning of these words.

For example, John 1:4 says, "In Him was life." In reading such a word we have to know the Old Testament background. In the beginning of the Old Testament, Genesis 2 says that after God made man He placed him before the tree of life. What exactly is the tree of life? What is the reason that God placed man before the tree of life? If you stop at Genesis 2, you will find it difficult to answer these questions. If you keep on reading, however, when you come to John 1, you see a sentence that says, "In Him was life." This means that the life related to the tree of life in Genesis 2, the life that was mysterious to man, was in Him. In the beginning was the Word, and in the Word was life.

One day this Word became flesh, or we may say that this Word who was God came into man. John says that this was God tabernacling among men. This also has an Old Testament background. In the Old Testament times, there was a tabernacle among the Israelites. Through the tabernacle God dwelt among the Israelites to supply their every need. It was from the God who dwelt in the tabernacle that the Israelites drew the supply to meet all their needs in the wilderness. The God in the tabernacle was their light; the God in the tabernacle was their revelation; the God in the tabernacle was their guidance; the God in the tabernacle was their supply. The God in the tabernacle was their source of everything. All their problems were solved by the God who dwelt in the tabernacle. When they were at war, the God in the tabernacle fought for them. When they had a lack, the God in the tabernacle came to supply them. Therefore, in the wilderness the Israelites received everything from the tabernacle. The God in the tabernacle met their every need. If there had not been a tabernacle, or if the God who dwelt in the tabernacle had departed from them, the Israelites would have had no solution for any problem, and they would have had no supply to meet any need.

Now the Word has become flesh; God has come into man. John says that this event was God tabernacling among men. Just as in the Old Testament the tabernacle among the Israelites was the center of God's union with man, so this tabernacle of God's becoming flesh is also the center of God's union with man. Just as in the Old Testament the tabernacle was the source of all supply to the Israelites, this tabernacle of God's becoming flesh is also the source of all supply to man. We need to have a substantial background in biblical knowledge to understand this point; otherwise, we will not have a thorough comprehension.

Second, Nathanael was amazed when he contacted the Lord because the Lord saw him under the fig tree before He met him. However, the Lord said, "You shall see greater things than these....You shall see heaven opened and the angels of God ascending and descending on the Son of Man" (1:50-51). I believe that by now, brothers and sisters, you know what the Lord Jesus was referring to. This is Jacob's dream becoming reality. One day Jacob was at Bethel, and in a dream he saw a ladder set up on the earth. Its top reached to heaven, and there the angels of God were ascending and descending on it (Gen. 28:12). Jacob said, "This is none other than the house of God" (v. 17). When he rose up in the morning, immediately he took the stone that he had put under his head, set it up as a pillar, and poured oil on top of it (v. 18). He said, "This stone, which I have set up as a pillar, will be God's house" (v. 22). If you impress this picture into your mind and then come again to read what the Lord Jesus said, you will clearly understand its meaning. What He said means that He is the ladder that Jacob saw in the dream. The incarnated Lord was to join earth to heaven and to open heaven to earth. The result of the joining of heaven and earth is that God gains a house on the earth.

This shows us that in the Gospel of John, the goal and result of the incarnation of God is that God is mingled with man to produce the house of God. The Lord's incarnation is the tabernacling of God among men. Therefore, the Lord Himself is a building of the mingling of God and man. The result of incarnation is that heaven is open to earth and earth is joined to heaven for God to be joined with man. This is Jacob's dream becoming a reality, so that God may gain a house on the earth.

Third, John 2 speaks of the Lord Jesus cleansing the temple. We know that the things in the Bible were not recorded in a casual way. The Lord Jesus did many things on the earth. Yet out of these many things, only those that have a special relationship with the truth that God wants to reveal were selected, recorded, and further depicted by the Holy Spirit. Because of this, we should believe that the Holy Spirit had a specific intention in recording the Lord Jesus' cleansing the temple in John 2.

In verse 18, after the Lord had cleansed the temple, the Jews asked Him, "What sign do you show us, seeing that you do these things?" The Lord Jesus answered and said, "Destroy this temple, and in three days I will raise it up" (v. 19). This was the only sign He would show them. Do you find this strange? Here the Lord Jesus spoke of Himself as the temple. What is this temple? It is God becoming flesh to enter into man and to be joined to man. Jesus the Nazarene was the temple. The Lord said, "Destroy this temple, and in three days I will raise it up." We all know that this refers to the Lord's resurrection. His incarnation was His tabernacling among men, so His body of flesh was the temple of God. The Jews would kill Him to destroy His body, but through His resurrection the Lord would rebuild His body that was destroyed by the Jews. In other words, He would rebuild the temple that was destroyed by the Jews. It is this tabernacle, this temple, that one day would cause the heaven to be opened and the angels of God to ascend and descend on Him. Therefore, John's record of these things is altogether for showing us that the Lord's incarnation, death, and resurrection were for the gaining of a tabernacle, a temple. Moreover, this tabernacle, this temple, is the house of God.

Regrettably, people rarely pay attention to these things when they read the Gospel of John. They may realize from reading the Gospel of John that in the Lord was life and that He came that men may have life. However, this is not enough. We need to further ask, "What is the purpose of life being in Him and of His coming that man may have life? What does He want to accomplish by being life and by entering into man to be life?" Brothers and sisters, I do not know if you have ever thought of this question. We have repeatedly said that He came into man as food to be man's life that man may enjoy Him. Now we need to ask, "What is the purpose of His coming into man to be life and to be enjoyed by man? What result does it produce?"

Previously we said that we were born a little more than a foot tall and weighed seven or eight pounds, but we have grown to be tall and big by being built up. How were we built up? It was by eating chicken, duck, fish, meat, rice, noodles, and vegetables. By eating and digesting day after day, slowly we grew to be as tall and heavy as we are today. Please remember, the digestion is the growth, the building. God's coming into us as food to be digested in us to be our life is likewise for the building up of His spiritual Body.

The Bible shows us that this Body is a house. In Ephesians the apostle, on the one hand, says that the church is the Body of Christ, and on the other hand, he says that the church is a spiritual house (1:22-23; 2:19-22). With us, our body is our house. Strictly speaking, we dwell in our body. In 2 Corinthians 5 the apostle tells us that our body is a temporary dwelling and that one day we will be clothed with a resurrected body, which is an eternal dwelling (vv. 1-3). When a person is about to leave this world, we often say that he is going away; he is leaving his body. This matches what the Bible means by saying that a body is a house. The church is the Body of Christ, and it is also the house of God. Therefore, the intention of God in coming into man as food, being digested in man, and being life to man is to build up the Body of Christ, that is, to build up His house.

The body the Lord put on in His incarnation was the body of one individual man, which was limited. However, the Body He built up after His death and resurrection is not limited to one individual man but includes all those who belong to Him throughout the generations and over the whole earth. If you understand that the story in the Gospel of John is outside of time and space, then you know that today the Lord Jesus is still here "resurrecting." I do not know if you understand this statement. This is to say that today the Lord Jesus is still here doing the work of resurrection. The temple destroyed by the Jews through Satan's instigation was only the Lord's body of flesh. But the temple He built up after His resurrection is an enlarged temple which includes all those who believe in Him throughout the ages and over the whole earth. Today this temple still is in the process of being built. That is why I said that the Lord is still doing the work of resurrection today.

Now we will see the purpose of the Lord's coming to be life as shown in the Gospel of John. He came to be life so that God and man may be joined as a building, a house. This house is the temple of God, the house of God. Although this is clearly shown in John, Regrettably when many read it, they do not easily see it. When people read expressions such as *tabernacle, destroy,* and *raise up* the temple in three days, and *heaven opened and the angels of God ascending and descending on the Son of Man,* it is very difficult for them to understand their meaning. After having this pointed out, I believe we all are very clear. John shows us that when God became a man

and came to be man's life, His intention was to have a tabernacle among men, and this tabernacle was God's temple.
Although this temple was destroyed, through His resurrection the Lord rebuilt the temple and enlarged it as well. This
temple is joined to heaven and causes heaven to be opened.
That was the scene at Bethel. Therefore, Christ's becoming
man's life is to build up Bethel, the house of God.

THE LORD BEING MAN'S LIFE
TO MEET MAN'S EVERY NEED
AND SOLVE ALL OF MAN'S PROBLEMS SO THAT MAN
MAY BE BUILT UP AS THE HOUSE OF GOD

Now we will take a look at the main point of each chapter
in the Gospel of John. We will first look at the first half of the
book, chapters one through thirteen. Chapter one is a general
outline, telling us in summary that the Lord was the Word in
the beginning. A person's words are his explanation; therefore, the Lord is the explanation of God, the expression of
God. No one has ever seen God; only He has declared God
(v. 18). In Him was life (v. 4). One day He became flesh and
tabernacled among men to bring life to man (v. 14).

Chapters two through thirteen show us how He meets
man's every need and solves all of man's problems. We need to
see that in the universe God wants to build Himself into man
and build man into Himself. God wants man to be His dwelling place, and He also wants man to take Him as his dwelling
place. However, the man whom God wants to build up to
become His dwelling has all kinds of needs and problems. I
would ask you brothers and sisters to consider this: God
wants to dwell in you as His dwelling place, and He also
wants you to dwell in Him as your dwelling place. However,
what kind of persons were you formerly? I believe we all have
to say from our heart that before we were saved, our true
condition was wretched. We were useless materials. Please
remember that after John gives us a general outline in chapter
one, he goes on in chapters two through thirteen to describe
how the man that God wants to build up is wretched and full
of needs and problems. He also speaks of how God became
man's life to meet man's needs and solve his problems.

Chapter two speaks about the first sign the Lord performed, which is the changing of water into wine. Here the wedding feast signifies the pleasure of human life, and the wine signifies man's life. Just as the pleasure of the wedding feast depends upon wine, so the pleasure of human life depends upon life. Just as the wine will run out, so man's life will come to an end and be finished. Therefore, John 2 tells us that the first condition of man is that his life will run out and come to an end. If you observe all the happenings among men, you will realize that the most miserable thing is that man's life runs out. Do you have a Ph.D.? One day your Ph.D. will still be here, but you will be gone. Maybe you are a millionaire; one day your riches will still be here, but you will be gone. Oh, there is an end to man's life! You may have many sons and daughters and many grandchildren, but one day your life will run out and be ended. This is man's first condition. Before we were saved, the first condition was that we were men whose life runs out.

There was a custom in my hometown that those who were wealthy would almost always have at least one top-quality coffin in their living room, prepared for the elderly ones in the family. When I was a child, coffins were the most frightening things to me, so I did not like going into others' living rooms. I cannot imagine the thoughts of those who have prepared a coffin for themselves when they see the coffin every day. Every day the coffin waits for them to come in and lie down.

This is the condition of human life. Man eats, drinks, and enjoys on the earth, attending a "wedding feast," but man is in death; his life will run out. Therefore, the Lord Jesus came to meet this need of man, to solve this problem. He used the sign of changing water into wine to reveal that He is the Lord of life. He is able to change the water of death into the wine of life. He is life, and He has come that man may have life (10:10). Therefore, in God's coming to be man's life, first He solves the problem of man's life running out.

Chapter three speaks about a moral man, a gentleman, one who feared God and endeavored to do good to please God. This is also a condition of man. I believe that many brothers and sisters were more or less in this kind of condition before. You tried to be virtuous and endeavored to do good. Although you would inevitably sin, at the same time you liked to do good to please God. However, the Lord who comes to be man's life shows us that this kind of doing good is useless. Man's problem before God is not a matter of doing good but a matter of being regenerated, receiving God into himself as life.

Therefore, regardless of how good a person is, he still needs to receive the life of God that he may be regenerated. It is not a matter of behavior but altogether a matter of life. It is not a matter of doing good or doing evil but a matter of whether or not one has received God as life to be regenerated. What man lacks is not behavior but life. Man's problem lies not in behavior without but in life within. God coming to be man's life is to solve man's problem of life.

Chapter four is a picture portraying thirst. We see a thirsty Lord asking for a drink and a thirsty sinner drawing water for a drink. The Lord is thirsty, and the sinner is also thirsty. This is another condition revealing that the man God desires to build is a thirsty person.

Everyone would agree that human life is a thirsty life. I believe that everyone has had this experience of being thirsty. If you were not thirsty, you would not have sought the Lord. In John 4 the Lord reveals that He is the living fountain. He is not Jacob's well. The water from Jacob's well cannot quench thirst; whoever drinks of it will thirst again. The Lord is the fountain of living water; whoever drinks of Him shall by no means thirst forever (vv. 13-14). God comes to be man's life so that those whom He builds will not thirst again, but the water He gives them will become in them a fountain of water gushing up into eternal life (v. 14).

Now we come to chapter five. In this chapter we see a man who had been thirty-eight years in his sickness, lying and unable to move. This was an impotent man who wanted to move but lacked the strength, being unable to achieve what he desired to do. This exposes the condition of man's impotence. I believe we all realize that we were the same way in the past. We truly desired to do good, but we could not do good. We really wanted to move, but we could not move. We were truly people who were paralyzed, paralytics who had been in that sickness for a long time. This is another condition of man. However, God comes into man to be man's life, causing one who is weak to become strong and one who cannot move to be able to move. Formerly we lay on the mat and were carried by the mat; now we carry the mat and walk back home.

How do we receive the Lord as life? We receive the Lord as life through His word. The Lord said, "The dead will hear the voice of the Son of God, and those who hear will live" (v. 25). To receive the word of the Son of God is to receive the Son of God Himself. Whoever receives the Son of God passes out of death into life. This causes the weak ones to become strong. Since death is the greatest weakness, when life comes in, weakness goes out.

Chapter six speaks of a crowd longing to be fed. This picture clearly portrays the condition of man's hunger. The Lord said, "I am the bread of life; he who comes to Me shall by no means hunger" (v. 35), "He who eats Me, he also shall live because of Me" (v. 57), and "The words which I have spoken to you are spirit and are life" (v. 63). These words tell us that if man receives and enjoys the Lord, he will be satisfied with food.

Chapter seven speaks about religion. The Jews were holding the Feast of Tabernacles, and on the last day of the feast, the Lord Jesus cried out, saying, "If anyone thirsts, let him come to Me and drink" (v. 37). This shows us that religion cannot quench man's thirst forever. While man may have a religion, a belief, and may joyfully participate in religious feasts, still there is a last day of the feast; there is an end. On the last day of the feast, the end of the feast, man is still thirsty. Therefore, the Lord said, "If anyone thirsts, let him come to Me and drink. He who believes into Me, as the Scripture said, out of his innermost being shall flow rivers of living water" (vv. 37-38). Not only is man himself no longer thirsty, but he can even quench others' thirst. This is another condition of man and the solution God brings by coming to be man's life.

Some brothers and sisters may have been religionists who

celebrated religious holidays such as Christmas and Easter. You might have felt very joyful while celebrating a feast, but when it ended, you felt that religion could not quench your thirst. Only the God who comes to be man's life can quench man's thirst within and even cause him to become rivers of living water, overflowing living water to satisfy and supply others.

Chapter eight gives the record of a sinful woman who committed the most immoral and defiling sin. The Jews said that according to the law of Moses, she should be stoned to death. This shows that the law condemns sinners to death. However, this God who comes to be man's life is able to save sinners from being slaves of sin. This is also a condition of man and the Lord's solution.

Chapter nine shows us another condition of man—blindness. Brothers and sisters, you should confess that in the past you were blind (I believe that you will not be offended by this). Each one of us used to live and flounder about blindly in this sinful world. We did not know God, and we did not know the eternal things. However, ever since the God who comes into man to be man's life came into us, He enlightened our inner eyes.

When the Lord opened the eyes of the blind man, He did it by anointing his eyes with spittle and clay and sending him to wash in the pool of Siloam, and he washed and came away seeing. In the past when I read that passage I did not understand the meaning; it seemed like a child's game. As I gradually came to understand the mingling of God and man, I understood what this meant. The clay is we human beings, because human beings are made of clay; we are all a clod of clay. What proceeds out of the Lord's mouth are His words, which are the Lord Himself. The Lord comes to mingle with us clay men. This is the mingling of God and man. This mingling causes us who are blind to be able to see.

Brothers and sisters, if within you there is no mingling with God, you will forever be blind. But when God Himself mingles with you, a clay man, through the words that proceed out from His mouth, your eyes are opened. Therefore, another condition of man is that he was born blind. There is the need for the God who comes to be man's life to enter into man, to mingle with man, so that man's eyes may be opened and enlightened.

Now we come to chapter ten. Chapter ten and chapter nine are related to the condition of man in two aspects. One aspect is his being blind; the other aspect is his being lost. Those who are blind are those who are lost; they are sheep without a shepherd. The Lord of life is the good Shepherd. The good Shepherd lays down His life for the sheep that the sheep might receive His life. He came that the sheep may have life. With any sheep that receives Him as life, on the one hand, his eyes are opened, being able to see, and on the other hand, he is returned to the flock to be under His hand, His shepherding.

I love hymn #44 in the Chinese hymnbook. The first stanza says that we bless the name of our Father as children taught by grace and we rejoice that because of His life we were brought back to the flock. This is exactly what John 10 says. Once His life comes into us, it causes us to return to the flock. We were formerly lost sheep; it was by His life coming into us that we became sheep belonging to the flock and being shepherded under the hand of the good Shepherd.

Chapter eleven speaks about a man who was sick and later died, was buried in the tomb, and even smelled. Yet the Lord who came to be man's life caused him to be raised from the dead, come out of the tomb, and be freed from all bondage. This tells us that the man God desires to build was formerly in death and in the tomb but is now enlivened by God entering into him.

Chapter twelve does not mention a particular condition of man. The main point in this chapter is a word spoken by the Lord: "Unless the grain of wheat falls into the ground and dies, it abides alone; but if it dies, it bears much fruit" (v. 24). The Lord in saying this tells us that He had to go through death and resurrection to impart His life to man, that is, to impart Himself as life into man, in order to meet all of man's needs as mentioned above.

Now we come to chapter thirteen. Chapter thirteen, which is a conclusion to the first half of the Gospel of John, shows us that the Lord, who comes to be man's life to solve all his problems and meet his every need, loves those who are His own and who receive His supply, and He cares for them to the uttermost. In this way they can become materials for His building to be built up by Him as His Body and the dwelling place of God.

This chapter starts by saying that the Lord, having loved His own who were in the world, loved them to the uttermost (v. 1). This means that He would bear all of their responsibilities. Then chapter thirteen goes on to relate the account of the Lord washing the feet of the disciples. This account reveals that He cares for those whom He loved, redeemed, regenerated, gained, and is building and bears their responsibility to the uttermost. If a person is willing to wash your feet, that is an indication that there is nothing else he would not do for you. This God who comes to be man's life cares for you and bears full responsibility for you. This is the content of chapter thirteen.

Now let us briefly reiterate. Chapter two tells us that man's life runs out; chapter three, that man needs to be born again; chapter four, that man is thirsty; chapter five, that man is impotent; chapter six, that man is hungry; chapter seven, that religion cannot quench man's thirst; chapter eight, that man lives in sin; chapter nine, that man is blind; chapter ten, that man is lost; chapter eleven, that man is dead; chapter twelve, that the Lord must impart His life to man; and chapter thirteen, that man needs the Lord's care and the Lord cares for man to the uttermost. These reveal the conditions and needs of the man whom God desires to build up.

Since the man whom God desires for His building is in such a condition, He needs to solve these problems and meet these needs for man. Thank the Lord that His coming to be man's life is to meet man's every need and solve all of man's problems. He can change the life that runs out into one that does not run out. Once He enters into man, He causes man to be regenerated. He alone is the living water that causes man to not thirst forever. He is also the bread of life that causes man to hunger nevermore. If a man lives by Him, He causes rivers of living water to flow out of his innermost being to water and satisfy others. He can make the weak strong. He releases and frees man from sin so that he is no longer a slave of sin. He gives sight to the blind and brings the lost back to His flock under His shepherding. He resurrects the dead and sets them free. He can do all of these things by imparting His life to man, and He cares for man to the uttermost, bearing all of man's responsibility.

In brief, therefore, the first half of the Gospel of John tells us that God came among men to be built together with men. The Lord's becoming flesh was His tabernacling among men. The Lord's body was the tabernacle. Later, the Lord Himself also said that His body was a temple, and although man would destroy the temple, He would raise it up again by His death and resurrection. Then the temple would be enlarged, not limited to Himself alone. In resurrection He comes into many people to be mingled with them; this is His building of the temple. However, since the people whom He is building are full of all kinds of problems, beginning from chapter three John shows us how He solves all of their problems and meets their every need by coming into them to be their life.

THE LORD'S GOING AND PREPARING A PLACE
BEING TO BRING MAN INTO GOD
TO BE BUILT TOGETHER WITH GOD
AS THE HOUSE OF GOD

Now let us look at the second half of the Gospel of John from chapter fourteen through chapter twenty-one. Starting with chapter fourteen the Gospel of John takes a turn. The center of the first half, composed of chapters one through thirteen, is God's becoming flesh and coming into man. The center of the second half, composed of chapters fourteen through twenty-one, concerns His "going." When the disciples heard the Lord say that He had to go, they were troubled. At the beginning of chapter fourteen, therefore, the Lord said, "Do not let your heart be troubled; believe into God, believe also into Me. In My Father's house are many abodes" (vv. 1-2). From here the Lord turned to the matter of abode.

We now need to address a very important question. What does *My Father's house* mentioned here refer to? We know this is not the first time that the Father's house is mentioned in the Gospel of John. As early as chapter two, when the Lord cleansed the temple, He said, "Do not make My Father's house a house of merchandise" (v. 16). Many brothers and sisters realize without difficulty that the Father's house in this verse refers to the temple at that time. Yet it is strange that when people come to the Father's house mentioned by the Lord in John 14, they think it refers to heaven. For two thousand years, many expositors of the Bible have interpreted this *Father's house* as heaven. Even many hymns in Christianity refer to God's house as heaven. In the Bible, whether the Old Testament or the New Testament, God's house and the Father's house are mentioned numerous times. The strange thing is this: Bible expositors agree unanimously that God's house in the Old Testament refers to the temple, while God's house in the New Testament refers to the church, yet the Father's house mentioned in John 14:2 is considered the unique exception and interpreted as heaven. This is indeed a strange thing.

Brothers and sisters, I wonder whether you still think that the Father's house is heaven when you read John 14:2. The Lord says, "In My Father's house are many abodes; if it were not so, I would have told you; for I go to prepare a place for you. And if I go and prepare a place for you, I am coming again and will receive you to Myself" (vv. 2-3). What does the Lord mean by *go?* How does He prepare a place for us? Where is this place? He says that He will come again to receive us. Does this *come again* refer to His second coming in the future? We should find answers to all these questions.

When I was young and newly saved, I heard a preacher speaking on John 14, which to this day has left in me a deep impression. He said, "The Lord told us that He would go and prepare a place for us, and when it is prepared, He would come again. This coming again will happen one day in the future. The Lord is now in the Father's house, and this Father's house is the heavenly mansion. He went there to prepare a room for every one of us who are saved. This is what the Lord meant by His going to prepare a place for us. When He has prepared the place, He will come again to receive us. The Lord has been gone for more than one thousand nine hundred years but has not returned to receive us, because the place has not been fully prepared. Oh, it has taken the almighty Lord more than one thousand nine hundred years, and yet the heavenly mansion has not been fully prepared! Can you imagine how extravagant and how magnificent that place will be? Therefore, we ought to thank and praise Him. Moreover, we do not need to build a very good house on the earth, for this is not our eternal dwelling place. Now the Lord is building a better house for us in heaven, and that will be our eternal abode." He spoke quite well and I listened enthusiastically.

Thirty years passed by, and under the Lord's leading I gradually came to understand the matter of the mingling of God and man. Because of this, when I read the Gospel of John again, I became very clear concerning the Lord's going to prepare the Father's house. I realized that "preparing a place" refers to the Lord's building of the church. Let me ask you brothers and sisters a question. In Matthew 16 the Lord Jesus said, "I will build My church" (v. 18). In John 14 the Lord Jesus said that He would prepare a house. Please consider how many buildings the Lord has in the universe. Does He have two buildings or just one building? Could it be that today the Lord is building the church on the earth and at the same time building a mansion in heaven as the house of God? Or is it that His building of the church is His building of the house of God? In other words, are the building of the church in Matthew 16 and the preparation of a place in John 14 two matters or one?

Those who agree with interpreting the Father's house in John 14 as heaven have a seemingly clear explanation. They say that the place the Lord is preparing is the city referred to in Hebrews 11 that Abraham, Isaac, and Jacob longed for, and it is also the holy city, New Jerusalem, mentioned in Hebrews 12 and Revelation 21. With this we agree. But we have to ask, "Is the holy city, the house of God, something apart from the church? Is it that today God is building the church on the earth as well as the holy city in heaven?" Dear brothers and sisters, can you believe that God has two buildings today? Five or six years ago, I asked the Lord in a serious way if He has two buildings in the universe. The answer I received was clearly negative. God has only one building in the entire universe. God will never build a mansion in heaven as His house. Rather, God is building His redeemed people as His house. God is not building a place; He is building Himself with those whom He redeemed. God is building Himself into man and man into Himself so that He and man can be mingled to become a house.

John clearly tells us that God's becoming flesh was His tabernacling among men, and the body of flesh that He put on was a tabernacle, which was also a temple. The Jews wanted to kill Him to destroy this temple, but He resurrected in three days, thereby rebuilding this temple and enlarging it to become an eternal temple. In John 2 the Lord clearly said that this temple is the Father's house. Please consider, in John 14 when the Lord again mentioned the Father's house, can this Father's house be heaven? It is very obvious that it absolutely does not refer to heaven. This Father's house refers to a spiritual house brought about by the mingling of God and man. You should be fully clear about this after you read John 14 through 17.

The Lord said, "In My Father's house are many abodes...for I go to prepare a place for you. And if I go and prepare a place for you, I am coming again and will receive you to Myself, so that where I am you also may be" (14:2-3). Where is the Lord? We have seen that the Lord clearly said that He is in the Father. Therefore, when the Lord said, "Where I am you also may be," He meant that He would cause us to also be in the Father. When the Lord spoke these words, the disciples, including Peter, James, and John, were not yet in the Father. Because of this, the Lord said that He would go to do something, which was to open a way, to prepare a place, to bring them into the Father. Therefore, we see that this preparing a place is to build man into God. The Lord seemed to be saying, "I am in God, but you are outside of God. Where I am today you cannot be. That is why I am going to prepare a place, and when it is prepared, I will come again to receive you to where I am so that where I am you also may be. I am going, and what I mean by *going* is that I am about to die. My death is to open a way for you and solve the problems between you and God. After I die, you will be able to draw near to God. Furthermore, My death enables you to come into God." Therefore, in saying that He would come again after preparing a place, the Lord was not at all referring to His second coming in the future.

Brothers and sisters, this is altogether different from the concepts we have received in the past from traditional Christianity. Therefore, we have to ask the Lord to grant us clear light. I also hope that we will read John 14, 15, 16, and 17 more thoroughly so that we all may see the central revelation of the Gospel of John: God tabernacles with man in order to build up the temple and fulfill Jacob's dream at Bethel so that He may have a building in the universe as the mutual dwelling place of God and man.

CHAPTER THREE

THE LORD'S BUILDING
THROUGH DEATH AND RESURRECTION

We have mentioned repeatedly that the Gospel of John shows us that God in His Son coming to be man's life was for Him to build a temple, which is His house. The Lord's becoming flesh was His tabernacling among men. His body of flesh was the tabernacle and also a temple. Later, Satan instigated the Jews to crucify Him on the cross, destroying this temple. Still, through resurrection, the Lord raised up the temple again in three days, thus enlarging it. When the Lord became flesh, He provided God with a tabernacle to dwell among men, yet this tabernacle was limited to only one individual. After the Lord resurrected and rebuilt the temple, it became boundless, no longer limited to one individual but including all those who have been regenerated in His resurrection and have received His life throughout the ages. Therefore, this building began with the Lord's incarnation and was eventually completed in the Lord's death and resurrection. The Lord completed this building, this temple, in resurrection.

When the temple was completed, heaven was opened to the temple. This was what the Lord referred to in John 1: "You shall see heaven opened and the angels of God ascending and descending on the Son of Man" (v. 51). We should realize that *the Son of Man* refers not only to the Lord Himself but also includes all those who are joined to Him in His resurrection. This Son of Man is a mysterious man in the universe. The angels of God ascending and descending on this man indicates that this man is joined to heaven and has reached the earth; heaven and earth are joined in Him; and God and man are mingled together in Him.

Brothers and sisters, if you will keep these points in mind and read John 14, 15, and 16—the chapters containing the Lord's parting message—and John 17 containing the Lord's concluding prayer, you will be able to understand the proper meaning. Simply speaking, the Lord was showing us that He would go through death and resurrection to accomplish the building of God.

THE LORD GOING TO BRING US INTO GOD

As we did previously, we will now read from John 14. Verse 2 says, "In My Father's house are many abodes; if it were not so, I would have told you." We have already pointed out that the writings of John do not have the element of space or time. Therefore, when reading them, we need to go beyond the concept of space and time. When John mentions time, it refers, in principle, to eternity; the space he speaks of is simply God Himself. The matters he deals with are all in eternity and also in God. Therefore, do not assume that the Father's house here refers to heaven or some other place. The Father's house mentioned here and in chapter two both refer to the mutual dwelling place of God and man. In this dwelling place there are many abodes. Later, we shall see what these abodes refer to.

"For I go to prepare a place for you" (v. 2). In John 14 and 16 the Lord repeatedly speaks about His going. The Lord's going does not refer to His leaving the earth to ascend to the heavens, but it refers to His going to die. I repeat: In the Gospel of John, we see that the Lord's becoming flesh is not just His coming from heaven to earth but His coming from God to man. His coming and going are not a matter of place but a matter of person. In the Gospel of John, in principle, there is no mention of place, only of person. Therefore, His incarnation was to bring God into man, and His death and resurrection were to bring man into God. In other words, His incarnation was His coming, and His death and resurrection were His going.

Since the Lord's going refers not to His leaving the earth to ascend to the heavens but to His death, His going to prepare a place for us must also not be His going to heaven but

His going into God to prepare a place, that is, His going to God to open a way for us, solving the problems and removing the barriers between us and God so that we who were outside of God and separated from God can enter into God and be joined to God. This is what the Lord meant by His going to prepare a place.

Thus, you can see that the Lord's word here has no thought of heaven at all. The Lord never meant to go to heaven to build a house for us, to prepare an abode for each of us, and having prepared it, to come again to receive us. This is altogether man's concept, not the Lord's intention. The Lord's intention was that He would go to suffer death, redeem us from our sins, terminate the flesh, deal with Satan, deal with the world, deal with all of the barriers, problems, and difficulties between us and God, and pave a way that we may be joined to God, enter into God, and dwell in God as our abode. This is what the Lord meant by His going to prepare a place for us. This shows us that God's salvation is not to save us into heaven but to save us into Himself in His Son. God is saving us not from earth to heaven but from ourselves into Himself.

Many times we do not preach the gospel accurately. In preaching the gospel to others, we often say, "Friends, do you know where you are going when you die? Where is your eternal home? If you do not believe in the Lord Jesus, you will go to hell. You can go to heaven only if you believe in Jesus." It is absolutely right to say that a person who does not believe in Jesus will go to the lake of fire. However, it is questionable to say that a person who believes in Jesus will go to heaven.

One time I was in a certain place giving a message concerning the building of God's house. I then asked the audience, "You are very familiar with the Bible and have received much light. Now I would challenge you and also challenge all of Christianity. Please tell me where the Bible says that those who believe in Jesus will go to heaven." I went on to say, "I know you will say in your heart that in John 14 when the Lord Jesus said, 'I go to prepare a place for you,' the place He was going to prepare must be heaven." Then I said, "We will temporarily put John 14 aside, saving it for a later time. But I would say that in the whole Bible you cannot find one place where it talks about people going to heaven."

A few days later, one of those who listened to the message that day invited us for a meal and fellowship. After the meal an elderly sister who was very familiar with the Bible asked me, "Brother Lee, since we are not in a hurry, can you speak to us from John 14, which you saved a few days ago?" I said, "Yes, but I would rather not merely speak on it. It is best if we read it together." So together we read over it briefly. When we came to "in My Father's house," I asked, "In the entire Bible, what does God's house or the Father's house refer to?" The sister said, "In the Old Testament it certainly refers to the temple of God, and in the New Testament it definitely refers to the church of God." Then I asked, "So what does the Father's house refer to in John 14?" She said, "Everyone believes that it refers to heaven." I immediately went on to say, "You just said that in the Old Testament God's house refers to God's temple and in the New Testament it refers to the church. Why is it that the Father's house in John 14 alone refers to heaven?" She said, "That is what everyone says, so I think it is probably so." I said, "Why is your thought not according to the Old Testament and the New Testament? Neither the Old Testament nor the New Testament says that God's house is heaven."

When we read further, I asked her, "The Lord Jesus said, 'For I go to prepare a place for you.' What did the Lord mean by the word *go?*" She said, "That certainly means that the Lord would leave the earth to ascend to the heavens." I asked, "What is meant by the phrase *prepare a place?*" She said, "Everyone says that it means that the Lord was going to heaven to build rooms for us." Therefore, I had to read on further with her little by little. It took me a great deal of effort to help her see that the Lord's going refers to His death, and His going to prepare a place was His going to solve the problems between us and God, to pave a way that we may be connected with God, joined to God, and dwell in God. Therefore, to be sure, the Lord's going to prepare a place for us is not for us to go to heaven but for us to enter into God.

THE LORD BEING IN THE FATHER
THAT WE ALSO MAY BE IN THE FATHER

"And if I go and prepare a place for you, I am coming again and will receive you to Myself" (v. 3). The meaning of the Greek words translated as *I am coming again* is difficult to render accurately. "If I go...I am coming" means "My going is My coming." Indeed, the Lord's going was His coming. In other words, the Lord's going to die was His going to be resurrected. From the perspective of death, it was His going; from the perspective of resurrection, it was His coming. Brothers and sisters, I do not know if you understand what I am saying. His going was His coming. Please keep this word in mind.

What the Lord was saying was, "My going is My coming." For what was His coming? He was coming to "receive you to Myself." He did not say to "receive you to where I am," that is, to a place. Rather, He said, "receive you to Myself," that is, into a person. Therefore, it is not a matter of going to a place but a matter of entering into a person. The Lord did not at all intend to receive us to a place, but rather to receive us into Himself.

Then the Lord said that "where I am you also may be." Where is the Lord? Is He in heaven? You will be clear after reading verse 20. There the Lord said, "I am in My Father." Therefore, what the Lord intends is to bring us into the Father. He is in the Father that we also may be in the Father. Since the Lord's going into death was to remove the barriers between us and God, to pave a way that we may be connected to God, joined to God, and also dwell in God, after the Lord went and finished the preparation, He came to receive us into Himself. In that day He was in the Father, and we also are in the Father, thus fulfilling His word, "Where I am you also may be."

Verse 4 says, "And where I am going you know the way." Where was the Lord going? Many would say, "He was going to heaven." However, it is a marvelous fact that the Gospel of John does not tell us that the Lord ascended to heaven. Brothers, do you see where the Lord was going? By now we should realize that He was going to the Father. In His incarnation He came out of the Father; now He was going into death and resurrection to go back into the Father. That is why I have repeatedly said that in John there is not the matter of place but only the matter of person.

The Lord said, "And where I am going you know the way." What is the way? Among the disciples there was Thomas, a doubtful person, who asked the Lord, "Lord, we do not know where You are going; how can we know the way?" Do you think that Thomas asked a foolish question? The strange thing is that today many people seem to be smarter than Thomas and are sure that the Lord was going to heaven. Today everyone seems to know what Thomas did not know back then! Regrettably, though, this presumptuous knowing prevents them from knowing what the Lord really meant.

What exactly is the way? The Lord Jesus said, "I am the way" (v. 6). So you see that this is altogether a matter of person. It is not that there is a physical way; the way is this One who is both God and man. There is not an actual place; the "place" is God Himself.

"I am the way and the reality and the life; no one comes to the Father except through Me" (v. 6). The Lord did not say, "No one comes to where the Father is"; rather, He said, "No one comes to the Father." What the Lord meant was, "No one can enter into the Father except through Me, the incarnated One." The Lord was not talking about going to where the Father is but going into the Father Himself. This going is not to a place but into a person.

Therefore, you can see that in the Gospel of John both the way and the place are a person. The way is the Son of God, and the place is God Himself. No man comes to God except through the Son of God. This was what the Lord meant. You may ask how we know that this was what the Lord meant. This is clear when we come to verse 20. Verse 20 says, "In that day you will know that I am in My Father, and you in Me, and I in you." Is this clear? What He accomplished in that day was not that He brought us to heaven but that He brought us into God. He Himself is the way that He might give us a passage into God. He saves us who are outside of God into God that we might have a union with God and dwell in Him. This is the meaning of John 14.

"If you had known Me, you would have known My Father also; and henceforth you know Him and have seen Him. Philip said to Him, Lord, show us the Father and it is sufficient for us" (vv. 7-8). A person is quite foolish before his inner eyes are opened by God. Philip did not know that the Lord with whom he was talking was the Father. Therefore, the Lord said to him, "Have I been so long a time with you, and you have not known Me, Philip? He who has seen Me has seen the Father; how is it that you say, Show us the Father? Do you not believe that I am in the Father and the Father is in Me?" (vv. 9-10). Brothers and sisters, where is the Lord? He clearly said that He is in the Father. But when the Lord spoke these words, He had not yet removed the barriers between us and God, solved the problems between us and God, or opened the way to God. Therefore, at that time the disciples were not yet able to enter into the Father. For this reason the Lord went to die that we might be together with Him in the Father. Then the word of the Lord would be fulfilled: "I am in My Father, and you in Me, and I in you."

THE HOLY SPIRIT COMING AS THE LORD IN ANOTHER FORM TO ENTER INTO US

Verses 10 through 17 say, "The words that I say to you I do not speak from Myself, but the Father who abides in Me does His works. Believe Me that I am in the Father and the Father is in Me; but if not, believe because of the works themselves. Truly, truly, I say to you, He who believes into Me, the works which I do he shall do also; and greater than these he shall do because I am going to the Father. And whatever you ask in My name, that I will do, that the Father may be glorified in the Son. If you ask Me anything in My name, I will do it. If you love Me, you will keep My commandments. And I will ask the Father, and He will give you another Comforter, that He may be with you forever, even the Spirit of reality, whom the world cannot receive, because it does not behold Him or know Him; but you know Him, because He abides with you and shall be in you." This section tells us that the Holy Spirit will be with us.

Verse 18 says, "I will not leave you as orphans; I am

coming to you." Amazingly, at this point the Lord's speaking took a turn. Verses 16 and 17 say that the Holy Spirit would come, and verse 18 says that the Lord Himself would come. Please keep in mind that the Holy Spirit is the Lord Himself. The "I" in verse 18 is the "He" in verse 17. Therefore, the Holy Spirit is the Lord's transfiguration, the Lord's changing into another form. This may be compared to vapor turning into water at a certain temperature, changing into another form, so that we may say that water is the transfiguration of vapor. If the temperature lowers to the freezing point, the water freezes into ice, which is the transfiguration of water, since it is in another form. Therefore, whether it is vapor, water, or ice, it is the same thing. This is a fitting illustration for explaining the God who is three yet one. The Son is the embodiment of the Father, and the Spirit is the transfiguration of the Son. On the one hand, there are the Father, the Son, and the Spirit; on the other hand, the Father, the Son, and the Spirit are one.

Please keep in mind that even though the Lord Jesus was God becoming flesh, He could be only among men; He could not get into man. He needed to be transfigured into the Holy Spirit in order to get into man. Once He was transfigured into the Holy Spirit, not only could He be among men to be with them, but He could also enter into them to dwell in them. This is why in chapter fifteen the Lord said several times that He would be in them and they in Him. When He was still in the flesh, He could only say, "I am in the midst of you," not "I am in you." Only after He was raised from the dead and transfigured into the Holy Spirit could He enter into man. This transfiguration of His is the "another Comforter" sent by God. This is like water melted from ice yet still being ice. We can say that ice and water are two things, but once the ice is melted, it is water. Likewise, although we can say that the Lord Jesus and the Holy Spirit are two, actually They are one.

To be transfigured, transformed, is to be changed from one form to another. Previously the Lord was in the flesh, but through death and resurrection He was transfigured into the Spirit. Therefore, in actuality the "another Comforter" is not another person but the same person transfigured into another form. Therefore, the "He" in verses 16 and 17 is the "I" in verse 18: "I will not leave you as orphans; I am coming to you."

"I am coming" here is hard to translate accurately. When the Holy Spirit inspired the writing of the Bible, His utterance was very particular in such places. The meaning in the original language is, "I will not leave you as orphans; My going is My coming." Therefore, this verse may be properly translated as, "I am coming to you" because the Lord's going was not His leaving them; His going was His coming. Furthermore, He was not coming to the place where they were, but coming into them. This also is not a matter of place but altogether a matter of person.

IN RESURRECTION THE LORD
JOINING MAN TO HIMSELF,
THUS ACCOMPLISHING GOD'S BUILDING

Verse 19 says, "Yet a little while and the world beholds Me no longer, but you behold Me." I would like to ask you, brothers and sisters, exactly how long is "a little while" mentioned here? Is it two thousand years? Is it until the time of the Lord's second coming? If it will be at that time, then the Lord could not say "the world beholds Me no longer" because at His second coming the whole world will behold Him. Therefore, here the Lord was obviously referring to His appearing to the disciples and His coming into their midst after His resurrection. How long would that little while be? It would be only three days! Therefore, the Lord said, "Yet a little while and the world beholds Me no longer, but you behold Me." Moreover, their beholding the Lord was first an outward beholding, and later it became an inward beholding, because after His resurrection the Lord not only appeared to them, coming into their midst, but He also entered into them, dwelling in them. The Lord's intention in appearing to them after His resurrection was to teach them to turn from knowing Him outwardly to knowing Him inwardly. It was only in this way that they could be mingled with the Lord.

The Lord went on to say, "Because I live, you also shall live." He was saying, "At the time of My resurrection, you will be regenerated because of Me; hence, because I live, you also shall live."

"In that day you will know that I am in My Father, and you in Me, and I in you" (v. 20). We need to stress "in that day." "In that day" means in the day of the Lord's resurrection. What would happen in that day? Did the Lord say, "In that day you will know that I have gone up to heaven"? Did He say, "In that day because I am in heaven, so I will save you also into heaven"? I believe by now, brothers and sisters, you are clear that it is not so. The Lord said, "In that day you will know that I am in My Father, and you in Me." Since the Lord is in the Father and we are in the Lord, we are also in the Father. This fulfills the Lord's word: "Where I am you also may be" (v. 3). Verse 20 has three *in*s, proving that all the mentions of *where* in chapter fourteen that seem to be referring to a place are altogether a matter of person.

Therefore, we can say boldly that in chapter fourteen there is not the matter of space or the matter of place but only the matter of person. The place in chapter fourteen is a person. The Lord seemed to be saying, "In that day you will know that I am in My Father, and you in Me, and I in you, so you and I are in the Father together." This is the fulfillment of, "Where I am you also may be." At this point God and man have a complete union.

I have repeatedly said that this union is the mingling of God and man—God is in man, and man is in God. This is also the building that God is building. This building is the mutual abode of God and man—God dwelling in man and man dwelling in God.

The Lord said, "Destroy this temple, and in three days I will raise it up" (2:19). This means that in His resurrection the Lord would build up the temple, which is the union of God and man. Therefore, the Lord seemed to say, "In that day, that is, in the day of My resurrection, because I live, you also shall live. Moreover, you will know that I am in My Father, and you in Me, and I in you." With these three *in*s, with the mingling and mutual indwelling of God and man, the Lord accomplished the building of the temple. This is what the Lord meant when He said that He was going to prepare a place for us, and when it was prepared, He would come and receive us to Himself. Previously, the disciples were outside of the Lord, but in that day they would be in the Lord; just as the Lord was in the Father, the Lord also would be in them.

THE LORD'S ABODE BEING
A GROUP OF PEOPLE WHO BELIEVE IN THE LORD
AND WHO LOVE HIM

Let us read on in chapter fourteen from verses 21 to 23: "He who has My commandments and keeps them, he is the one who loves Me; and he who loves Me will be loved by My Father, and I will love him and will manifest Myself to him. Judas, not Iscariot, said to Him, Lord, and what has happened that You are to manifest Yourself to us and not to the world? Jesus answered and said to him, If anyone loves Me, he will keep My word, and My Father will love him, and We will come to him and make an abode with him." *Abode* here and *abodes* in verse 2—"in My Father's house are many abodes"—are the same word in Greek. In verse 2 it is plural, but here it is singular. At this point you can realize that the abodes mentioned in verse 2 are a group of people who love the Lord, fellowship with the Lord, and live in the Lord, and to whom the Lord manifests Himself, as seen in verses 21 through 23. *Abodes* in verse 2 cannot refer to another entity—heaven—because they are mentioned in the same chapter of the Bible and in the same message given by the Lord Jesus. Therefore, we can say with certainty that the abodes do not refer to a place but to a person. The abodes are the group of people who believe in the Lord, love the Lord, have fellowship with the Lord, live in the Lord, and allow the Lord to manifest Himself to them and dwell together with them. This group of people is the many abodes in the Father's house.

Let us read further. "Jesus answered and said to him,...He who does not love Me does not keep My words; and the word which you hear is not Mine, but the Father's who sent Me. These things I have spoken to you while abiding with you; but the Comforter, the Holy Spirit, whom the Father will send in My name, He will teach you all things and remind you of all the things which I have said to you. Peace I leave with you;

My peace I give to you; not as the world gives do I give to you. Do not let your heart be troubled, neither let it be afraid. You have heard that I said to you, I am going away and I am coming to you. [This is the third time the Lord said that His going was His coming]. If you loved Me, you would rejoice because I am going to the Father, for the Father is greater than I. And now I have told you before it happens, so that when it happens you may believe" (vv. 23-29).

Brothers and sisters, let me ask you, according to the context, what was the thing that would happen when the Lord said, "When it happens you may believe"? Was it that the Lord would ascend to heaven? No, if you read from chapter fourteen through chapter twenty, you will see that the Lord was referring to His being resurrected from the dead to bring man into God and to bring Himself into man. When this would happen, the disciples would believe.

Now we go on to verses 30 and 31: "I will no longer speak much with you, for the ruler of the world is coming, and in Me he has nothing; but this is so that the world may know that I love the Father, and as the Father commanded Me, so I do. Rise, let us go from here."

THE LORD BRINGING US INTO THE FATHER
THAT HE MAY BE UNITED WITH US
AND ABIDE WITH US MUTUALLY

By now I believe that you have understood the words in John 14. Let us go on to read chapter fifteen, which immediately follows chapter fourteen. "I am the true vine, and My Father is the husbandman. Every branch in Me that does not bear fruit, He takes it away; and every branch that bears fruit, He prunes it that it may bear more fruit. You are already clean because of the word which I have spoken to you. Abide in Me and I in you. As the branch cannot bear fruit of itself unless it abides in the vine, so neither can you unless you abide in Me. I am the vine; you are the branches. He who abides in Me and I in him, he bears much fruit; for apart from Me you can do nothing" (vv. 1-5).

Because chapter fourteen already says that one day something in particular would happen—that the Lord would be resurrected from the dead and bring us into God, and that He Himself would also abide in us—in chapter fifteen there is the fact of the union of the vine and branches. The fact that we can abide in the Lord and the Lord can abide in us so that He and we can have a mutual abode is altogether the result of the Lord's going and coming—His death and resurrection in chapter fourteen. Without the events in chapter fourteen, there cannot be the fact in chapter fifteen. The fact in John 15 is that we abide in the Lord and the Lord abides in us. Our union and mingling with the Lord is the same as the union of the branches with the vine. This union makes it possible for God and man to have a mutual abode and thereby accomplish the building of God.

That is why I repeatedly say that in chapter fourteen the Father's house does not refer to heaven, and the many abodes do not refer to many rooms in heaven. The Father's house refers to the building of God in the universe, and the many abodes are people who are mingled with God and who abide in God. Everyone who is mingled with God and abides in God is an abode in which God abides. At the same time, God is their abode because they abide in God. Only when we come to chapter fifteen do we have the utterance concerning mutual abiding: "Abide in Me and I in you" (v. 4).

THE HOLY SPIRIT COMING
TO BRING US INTO THE REALITY OF THIS UNION

Let us leave for now the remainder of chapter fifteen and read from chapter sixteen. Verses 5 through 7a say, "But now I am going to Him who sent Me; and none of you asks Me, Where are You going? But because I have spoken these things to you, sorrow has filled your heart. But I tell you the truth, It is expedient for you that I go away; for if I do not go away, the Comforter will not come to you." The Lord's meaning was, "If I do not go, I cannot be transfigured to enter into you. My going is expedient for you. If I do not go, I can be only among you but cannot enter into you." Verses 7b-13a continue, "But if I go, I will send Him to you. And when He comes, He will convict the world concerning sin and concerning righteousness and concerning judgment: Concerning sin, because they do not believe into Me; and concerning righteousness, because I am going to the Father and you no longer behold Me; and concerning judgment, because the ruler of this world has been judged. I have yet many things to say to you, but you cannot bear them now. But when He, the Spirit of reality, comes, He will guide you into all the reality." The Spirit of reality is the Lord's transfiguration. He does not guide us into doctrines but into all the truth, all the reality. What is all the reality? It is, "I am in My Father, and you in Me, and I in you" (14:20). This is for man to fully enjoy everything that is in God, which is also to enter into reality.

John 16:13b-15 says, "For He will not speak from Himself, but what He hears He will speak; and He will declare to you the things that are coming. He will glorify Me, for He will receive of Mine and will declare it to you. All that the Father has is Mine; for this reason I have said that He receives of Mine and will declare it to you." This is a very great word, but I cannot go into its details at this time. The Lord Jesus was saying, "All that the Father is and has is Mine. When the Spirit of reality comes, He will guide you into all the reality, into all the fullness of the Godhead, so that you may enjoy all that is in the fullness."

THE LORD'S GOING REFERRING TO HIS DEATH, AND THE LORD'S COMING REFERRING TO HIS RESURRECTION

Verse 16 says, "A little while and you no longer behold Me, and again a little while and you will see Me." Brothers and sisters, I believe you know that when the Lord said this He was about to die. Therefore, He said, "A little while and you no longer behold Me" because He would be killed and buried. He also said, "And again a little while and you will see Me" because He would be resurrected as the Spirit to come into the midst of the disciples and also to enter into them.

Verses 17 and 18 continue, "Some of His disciples then said to one another, What is this that He says to us, A little while and you do not behold Me, and again a little while and you will see Me; and, Because I am going to the Father? Therefore they said, What is this that He says, A little while?

We do not know what He is talking about." The Lord said, "I am going to the Father"; this still refers to that mysterious event, and that was why the disciples did not understand it.

Verses 19 and 20 say, "Jesus knew that they wanted to ask Him and He said to them, Are you inquiring among yourselves concerning this, that I said, A little while and you do not behold Me, and again a little while and you will see Me? Truly, truly, I say to you that you will weep and lament, but the world will rejoice; you will be sorrowful, but your sorrow will be turned into joy." This refers to the period of time when the Lord was crucified and buried. During that time the Lord's followers would weep and be sorrowful, but the world that crucified the Lord would rejoice. Yet after the Lord's resurrection, the disciples would see the Lord and be joyful.

Verse 21 says, "A woman, when she gives birth, has sorrow because her hour has come; but when she brings forth the little child, she no longer remembers the affliction because of the joy that a man has been born into the world." The time the Lord Jesus went to die was the time the disciples would suffer birth pangs. Likewise, the time the Lord Jesus resurrected from death was the time the disciples would rejoice.

Verse 22 continues, "Therefore you also now have sorrow; but I will see you again and your heart will rejoice, and no one takes your joy away from you." The Lord's seeing the disciples again is not at the time of His second coming but in the day of His resurrection.

John 20:19 says, "When therefore it was evening on that day, the first day of the week, and while the doors were shut where the disciples were for fear of the Jews, Jesus came and stood in the midst and said to them, Peace be to you." This took place on the evening of the day of the Lord's resurrection. The doors were shut, yet Jesus came in; how He came, we do not know. Verse 20 continues, "And when He had said this, He showed them His hands and His side. The disciples therefore rejoiced at seeing the Lord." He did not come to the disciples merely as a soul or as a spirit; He came with a physical body that still bore the marks and wounds of crucifixion. Here you can see that the words in chapter sixteen are fulfilled in chapter twenty. In chapter sixteen the Lord said that He was going to die and the disciples would be sorrowful, but that would be only temporary, for when He would be resurrected and would see them again, they would be joyful. Then in the evening of the day of the Lord's resurrection, the Lord did come into the midst of the disciples, and the disciples saw Him and rejoiced.

I point out these verses to prove that *coming* in John 14 through 16 does not refer to the Lord's second coming in the future but refers to the Lord's coming into the midst of the disciples after His resurrection. Likewise *going* in these three chapters also refers not to the Lord's leaving the earth to ascend to heaven but to His death. His going refers to His death; His coming refers to His resurrection.

Let us continue by reading 16:22-25: "No one takes your joy away from you. And in that day [that is, the day of the Lord's resurrection] you will ask Me nothing. Truly, truly, I say to you, Whatever you ask the Father in My name, He will give to you. Until now you have asked for nothing in My name; ask and you shall receive, that your joy may be made full. These things I have spoken to you in parables; an hour is coming when I will no longer speak to you in parables, but I will report to you plainly concerning the Father." Please take note that the Lord reported to us plainly not concerning heaven but concerning the Father.

Verses 26 through 28 continue, "In that day you will ask in My name, and I do not say to you that I will ask the Father concerning you, for the Father Himself loves you, because you have loved Me and have believed that I came forth from God. I came forth out from the Father and have come into the world; again, I am leaving the world and am going to the Father." Here He is saying that He came forth from God and now was going back to God. All who read the Greek New Testament know that *world* in verse 28 is the same as *world,* that is, the people of the world, in 3:16. Here, therefore, *into the world* can be translated as "to the people of the world." He came forth out from the Father to the people of the world; this means that He came from God to man. Then He left the people of the world and went to the Father. This means that He went from man to God.

Verses 29 and 30 say, "His disciples said, Behold, now You are speaking plainly and not saying any parable. Now we know that You know all things and have no need that anyone ask You; by this we believe that You came forth from God." What a pity! The disciples had not believed until now that the Lord came forth from God; they had believed too late. Now it was not a matter of His coming forth from God but of His going back into God. Even now they had understood only the first part but not the second part. We need to keep in mind that the first section of John is about God coming into man, and the second is about man entering into God. When the Lord said these words, the disciples did not understand. Only until the evening of the day of the Lord's resurrection did they understand. Likewise, today if we do not see the fact, we cannot understand. Only when we see the fact can we understand. Now the disciples understood that the Lord came forth from the Father, yet they still did not understand how the Lord was going back to the Father.

Verses 31 through 33 conclude, "Jesus answered them, Do you now believe? Behold, an hour is coming, and has come, that you will be scattered each to his own place and will leave Me alone; yet I am not alone, because the Father is with Me. These things I have spoken to you that in Me you may have peace. In the world you have affliction, but take courage; I have overcome the world."

A CONCLUDING WORD

We will end our reading here. Now let us speak a concluding word. John 14, 15, and 16 speak about the Lord's coming by going, and this coming by going is His death and resurrection. Please remember that in this book, the Gospel of John, the first section speaks of the Lord's incarnation, and the second section speaks of the Lord's death and resurrection. In His incarnation He came forth from the Father into man; in His death and resurrection He went forth from man into the Father. In other words, through incarnation He brought God into man, and through death and resurrection He brought man into God. Through incarnation He brought God into a union with man, while through death and resurrection He brought man into the mingling with God. Therefore, from chapter one to chapter thirteen He could only say, "I am in your midst" and could not say, "You are in Me and in the Father." He could not say this word at that time because He had not brought man into God. Between God and man there were still barriers, distance, problems, and difficulties. These problems were sin, the world, the flesh, and Satan. Up until that time, the door for man to enter into God had not been opened. The way had not been paved, and there was not a way for man to abide in God.

Therefore, He had to go and die. He had to solve the problems between God and man through death. He had to pave a way and open up a way for man to reach God and abide in God. This was His going to prepare a place for man. He did not go to prepare a heavenly mansion for man to live in. Rather, He went through death to solve the problems between God and man, to open a way that man may have access to God and abide in God.

After His resurrection, the Lord as the Spirit imparted His life to man. That was His entering into man. At the same time, in His resurrection He brought the man He had put on into God. This fulfilled the word of the Lord that where He is those who belong to Him also may be. He is in the Father, and those who belong to Him are also in the Father. In this way God and man are mingled and united to become a spiritual building as the mutual abode of God and man, which is the house of God, the temple of God. This is accomplished through His resurrection. This also fulfills His word: "Destroy this temple, and in three days I will raise it up" (2:19). Today He is still building this temple in resurrection. He has been doing this building work in us with His resurrection life that we may enter more into God and deeper into God. This is the building work shown in the Gospel of John.

CHAPTER FOUR

THE LORD'S PRAYER FOR THE ONENESS AND THE BUILDING OF GOD AND MAN

We have already mentioned that John 14, 15, and 16 are a message given to the disciples by the Lord on the night of His betrayal after His supper was established. Then in John 17 the Lord offered a prayer to conclude the message. I believe that after the previous messages you brothers and sisters are very clear that in these three chapters—John 14, 15, and 16—the emphasis of the Lord's message is to show us how He would die to solve the problems between us and God and open a way for us to be connected to God, enter into God, and abide in Him. Furthermore, He would resurrect from death to impart His life to us that we may live as He lives, causing us to be able to abide in Him and He in us. In brief, the subject of His message is that He would bring man into God so that God and man would be fully built together to become one entity.

After He finished speaking the message, the Lord offered a prayer as a conclusion. We all have had such an experience. The concluding prayer we offer when we have finished speaking a message is often the central thought of the message. It is the same with the Lord's prayer on that occasion. In His prayer He brought the central thought of the message before God, asking God to fulfill it. If we know this, then this prayer can be more easily understood.

THE LORD ENTERING INTO GOD AND MANIFESTING GOD'S GLORY

Now we will read this prayer. John 17:1 says, "These things Jesus spoke, and lifting up His eyes to heaven, He said, Father, the hour has come; glorify Your Son that the Son may glorify You." This is the subject of the prayer. The subject of this prayer is that God would glorify His Son that His Son may also glorify Him. What is glory? We confess that even today we do not fully understand it. All the Bible expositors and those who pursue spiritual experience admit that glory is very difficult to explain. We have said before that glory is the manifestation, the expression, of God. God manifested and expressed is glory. This explanation is relatively simple and accurate. For example, when electricity shines forth and is manifested from within a light bulb, the shining is the glory of electricity. The fluorescent lamps here are the electricity shining forth. This shining is the glory of the electricity, which is also the manifestation, the expression, of electricity. This is a little illustration to help us to comprehend the meaning of glory. What is God's glory? God's glory is God's manifestation, God's expression. Whoever bears the expression of God has the glory of God. If you sense that a meeting is full of God's presence, then the meeting is full of God's glory.

Therefore, it is not difficult for us to understand what the Lord meant when He said, "Glorify Your Son." We need to keep in mind that the Lord's becoming flesh was God's entering into man. God Himself is glorious, but we human beings are not glorious; we are lowly and base. Therefore, the glory of God was concealed in the man whom God had become. In the tabernacle in the Old Testament, God's glory, or we may say God Himself, was concealed within a veil in the Holy of Holies. Hebrews 10 says that the veil typifies the flesh the Lord put on in His incarnation (v. 20). When the Lord became flesh, His flesh, His humanity, was a veil that concealed God's glory. Although the incarnated Lord was inwardly God Himself and absolutely glorious, He appeared before men outwardly as a lowly man. While He was in the flesh, in His dealings with men, His glory was not perceived, because it was hidden within Him. What people felt and touched in Him was a lowly man. Philippians 2 tells us that He humbled Himself, lowered Himself, taking the form of a slave, becoming in the likeness of men (v. 7). Therefore, when He appeared before men, He had no attracting form nor majesty that they should desire Him (Isa. 53:2). In man's eyes He was merely a man whose visage and form were marred. His glory was fully concealed, veiled, within His flesh.

Recall the time when the Lord Jesus went up the mountain with three disciples and was transfigured before their eyes. That was the release of the glory from within Him. His flesh as a veil seemed to have become transparent, letting out the glory within Him. However, that was only for a short while; afterward, His glory was concealed again, and the lowly form reappeared. In His thirty-three and a half years on the earth, what was expressed was His lowly form, not His glory.

Now in John 17 the Lord offered a prayer before God, saying, "Glorify Your Son." It is not difficult for us to understand the meaning of this word, which was to ask God to bring His Son fully into glory that His Son may fully manifest and express God's nature and God's glory. This was concerning His resurrection. When He was on the earth, He was the Son of God and had God within Him, but people always saw Him as a lowly man. However, He was not the same after resurrection. Once He resurrected, the glory within Him was manifested. Once He resurrected, the God within Him, the life of the Son of God within, was expressed. When He resurrected, His flesh was transfigured from a lowly form to a glorious form. Therefore, Luke 24 tells us that the Lord's resurrection was His entering into glory (v. 26).

Brothers and sisters, for God to become flesh and enter into man was to be made lowly; for man to enter into God was to be glorified. It was lowliness for the Lord Jesus to become flesh and bring God into man, but it was glory for the Lord Jesus to be resurrected and bring man into God. Now the Lord would go and die; that is, He would go through death and resurrection, so He offered a prayer, asking God to glorify Him, to cause Him to be glorified. This means that He asked God to cause all that was hidden within Him—God's life, God's nature, and all that God is—to be manifested and expressed. In Him was all the fullness of the Godhead, the very God Himself. When He was in the flesh, the fullness of the Godhead was concealed within Him. His humanity and His body, as a veil, concealed and confined all the fullness of God. Now His going to die was to split open the veil. After He died, He would be resurrected, causing the "veil" to be transfigured. By the splitting and the transfiguration of the veil, He would fully shine forth all the fullness of the Godhead that was previously hidden in Him. The result would be His glorification. Therefore, when He prayed to the Father, "Glorify Your Son," what He meant was, "May You cause all the fullness of the Godhead to be manifested and expressed from within Your Son."

Once you understand this phrase, you will understand the following clause: "That Your Son may glorify You." This is to say, "If You glorify Your Son in this way, Your Son will also glorify You. Since all that You are and have are in Your Son, if this veil of flesh is not broken, not transfigured, then Your glory will be confined within it. Now glorify Your Son that all of Your fullness may shine out from within Your Son. In this way You will glorify Your Son, and Your Son will also glorify You because all of Your fullness will be expressed through Your Son."

THE LORD GIVING MAN ETERNAL LIFE
THAT MAN MAY KNOW GOD

John 17:2 says, "Even as You have given Him authority over all flesh to give eternal life to all whom You have given Him." We admit that this prayer of the Lord contains many great expressions. We do not have time to cover them one by one, and some we cannot cover thoroughly. For instance, the glory we have just spoken of and the eternal life here are both very great items.

Verse 3 continues, "And this is eternal life, that they may know You, the only true God, and Him whom You have sent, Jesus Christ." This eternal life has a particular function within man, which is to cause man to know the only true God and Jesus Christ, whom God has sent. This eternal life within man has the function to cause him to know God and Christ; hence, it is related to the glory of the Son of God and the expression of God Himself as well.

Verse 4 says, "I have glorified You on earth, finishing the work which You have given Me to do." This word is hard to understand. I would like to ask you, brothers and sisters, to what does the Lord refer when He says that He glorified the Father while He was on earth, finishing the work which He gave Him to do? We can explain it this way: The Lord Jesus did many things on earth, and everything was done according to God's will. However, here the work which God had given Him to do refers specifically to the Lord's expressing God on the earth. "No one has ever seen God; the only begotten Son, who is in the bosom of the Father, He has declared Him" (1:18). "He who has seen Me has seen the Father" (14:9). These words indicate that God sent the Lord to the world with the intention of expressing Himself. The Lord came to the earth to declare God, explain God, express God, and impart God to man. In so doing, the Lord glorified the Father. Therefore, the Lord said that He had finished the work which the Father had given Him to do.

John 17:5 says, "And now, glorify Me along with Yourself, Father, with the glory which I had with You before the world was." The Lord seemed to be saying, "Previously I was with You, but when I became flesh, I came out from You into the world. Now I ask you to take Me back that I may participate in the glory along with You, in the glory which I had with You before the world was."

THE LORD MANIFESTING GOD'S NAME TO MAN

Verse 6a says, "I have manifested Your name to the men whom You gave Me out of the world." The name here is another great item. In this chapter we see three great items. The first item is glory; the second, life; and the third, the name. What did the Lord mean when He said, "I have manifested Your name to the men..."? We know that the name denotes the person; the name is the person. That the Lord manifested the Father's name to the disciples means that He manifested the Father to them. The Lord not only gave them the eternal life, but He also manifested the Father's name to them that they might know who the Father was.

THE LORD GIVING GOD'S WORDS TO MAN

Verses 6b through 8 continue, "They were Yours, and You gave them to Me, and they have kept Your word. Now they have come to know that all that You have given Me is from You, for the words which You gave Me I have given to them, and they received them and knew truly that I came forth from You, and they have believed that You sent Me." By now the disciples understood that the Lord came forth from God, but they still did not understand that the Lord was going back into God. By now the disciples knew that the Lord was the incarnated One, but they still did not understand that the Lord would also be the One who died and resurrected. Now they truly knew that the Lord came forth from the Father and was sent by the Father.

Verses 9 and 10a say, "I ask concerning them; I do not ask concerning the world, but concerning those whom You have given Me, for they are Yours; and all that is Mine is Yours, and Yours Mine." The beginning of verse 10, which says, "All that is Mine is Yours, and Yours Mine," is a great utterance. This is a matter of oneness. If you can tell the Lord, "All that is mine is Yours," then you can also tell Him, "All that is Yours is mine." This is similar to the relationship of a husband and wife. Because the husband and wife have become one, all that the wife has belongs to the husband, and all that the husband has belongs to the wife.

Verse 10b says, "And I have been glorified in them." This means that because the disciples belonged to the Lord, the Lord was then expressed and glorified. Then verse 11 begins, "And I am no longer in the world; yet they are in the world, and I am coming to You." The disciples did not understand this word yet. They understood only the first half, that is, that the Lord came forth from the Father. This verse ends with, "Holy Father, keep them in Your name, which You have given to Me, that they may be one even as We are." The name God gave to the Lord is a very great item. The Lord asked that those who belonged to Him be kept by God in the name God gave to Him, in order that they might become one even as the Triune God is one.

Verses 12 through 16 continue, "When I was with them, I kept them in Your name, which You have given to Me, and I guarded them; and not one of them perished, except the son of perdition [Judas], that the Scripture might be fulfilled. But now I am coming to You, and these things I speak in the world that they may have My joy made full in themselves. I have given them Your word, and the world has hated them, because they are not of the world even as I am not of the world. I do not ask that You would take them out of the world, but that You would keep them out of the hands of the evil one [Satan]. They are not of the world, even as I am not of the world." *Your word* in verse 14 is another great item; glory, life, the name, and the word are four great items.

THE GLORY OF GOD, THE ETERNAL LIFE, THE NAME OF GOD, AND THE WORD OF GOD BRINGING THE BELIEVERS INTO THE ONENESS AMONG THEMSELVES IN GOD AND INTO THEIR ONENESS WITH GOD

Verses 17 through 20 say, "Sanctify them in the truth; Your word is truth. As You have sent Me into the world, I also have sent them into the world. And for their sake I sanctify Myself, that they themselves also may be sanctified in truth. And I do not ask concerning these only, but concerning those also who believe into Me through their word." *These* refers to the disciples who were with the Lord that day. *Those also who believe into Me through their word* refers to all those who would believe the Lord through the gospel preached by the disciples throughout the ages. This includes all who would be saved at all times and in all places. Therefore, the Lord's prayer here is for all who have been saved and who belong to Him. Verse 21 continues, "That they all may be one; even as You, Father, are in Me and I in You, that they also may be in Us; that the world may believe that You have sent Me." How could the disciples be in "Us," that is, in the Lord and the Father? It was by the Lord's giving them the Father's eternal life, by the Lord's manifesting the Father's name to them, by the Lord's making known to them the word of God, the truth of God, and their receiving it, and by the Lord's giving them the glory which God gave Him. Through these four items—the eternal life, God's name, God's word, and God's glory—all those who belong to the Lord were brought into God. Through the eternal life, which is the life of God Himself, we are in union with God.

Through God's name as God's explanation, we can know God; that is, we can know what kind of God He is. Through God's word we are separated, set apart, from the world. Through God's glory we are fully brought into God. When we are fully in God, that is glory. Therefore, you must see these four items. God's life brings us into a union with God; God's name makes God known to us; God's word separates us from the world; and God's glory brings us fully into God. These four items not only bring all of us who belong to the Lord into absolute oneness, but they also bring us fully into the Triune God.

I cannot expound this portion verse by verse and sentence by sentence, but here I need to speak again about these four items: the eternal life, God's name, God's word, and God's glory. Please remember that all of us who belong to the Lord have the eternal life in us. This is why we can fellowship with one another, as 1 John 1:2 and 3 says, "We...report to you the eternal life...that you...may have fellowship with us." In the eternal life there is something called fellowship. The eternal life entering into you, into me, and into everyone who belongs to the Lord brings us all into fellowship.

On the other hand, God's name causes us to know what kind of God He is. The more you know God, the more you are in union with God's children. Furthermore, God's word, God's truth, separates us from the world outwardly. The more you know God's word, understand God's word, and comprehend God's truth, the more you come out of the world and the more you are separated from the people in the world. The more someone understands God's word and has God's speaking, the clearer the separating line is between him and the world. On the contrary, the more you blend with the world, the more you are separated from the children of God. The more you blend with the world, the more difficult it becomes to be in harmony with the brothers and sisters. The more you are separated from the world, the more you are drawn towards God's children, and the more you are in harmony with them.

Lastly, there is God's glory as well. If you are fully in God, in the glory of God, you will be absolutely one with God's children. In other words, if every one of us who belongs to the Lord lives in the fellowship of God's life, knows God's name, knows God Himself, receives God's word, and learns to live in God's glory, then we all are living in God. If so, do you think it is possible to not have oneness among us? It is impossible. On the contrary, if you and I do not live in the fellowship of the divine life, have a thorough knowledge of God, and sufficiently receive the word of God; if we instead blend, mix, with the world, and if at the same time we do not live in God or in God's glory, do you think we can be one? If we are such persons, surely we are isolated and separated from the saints. What isolates us? The world isolates us, not knowing God isolates us, and our self isolates us. These various isolations prevent God from building us.

For example, we may build a house with reinforced concrete. If the gravel is not thoroughly washed when we mix the concrete, the concrete will not be solid. Likewise, if we have the stains of the things of the world on us or the things of the self, then we will not be able to mingle with God's children. If we have all kinds of problems, we cannot be built together with God's children.

Therefore, for the church to be built up, merely exhorting the brothers and sisters to be one or praying to the Lord for them to be one will not make them one. This is not the way. We need to help them know the eternal life that is in them. We need to help them know the name of God and who God is. We need to lead them to read and receive the word of God, the truth of God. And we also need to lead them to live in God. In this way, you do not even have to speak about being one; the brothers and sisters will surely be one. This is the meaning of the Lord's prayer. The Lord's prayer shows us how we can be one, how we can be built up as one with all the saints. This building, this oneness, is not merely the oneness between men, but it is a oneness accomplished through everyone being in God and mingling together with God. This oneness of God and man is the building we are talking about.

Brothers and sisters, this building is accomplished by the Lord's resurrection. The Lord said, "Destroy this temple, and in three days I will raise it up" (John 2:19). Here the Lord was saying, "You destroy this temple with the death of the cross, but I will raise it up with resurrection life." This temple built with resurrection life is a building that is accomplished in God by those who are regenerated and who are living in Christ, being absolutely one with God.

If we are absolutely one in God in such a way, the world will believe that the Lord is the Christ sent by God. The power of the gospel is right here. If we are to lead others to know Christ, know the Lord, we must have this testimony of oneness. You can go and observe; wherever the brothers are not in one accord, in harmony, there is no power of the gospel. The gospel continues to be preached, but not many are saved, and those who are saved are not very strong and prevailing. If you want to preach a prevailing and strong gospel that man may know Christ and know that He is the One sent by God and the Lord appointed by God, then you must have a church that is in oneness, a church that is built up.

THE LORD BRINGING MAN INTO THE FATHER THAT MAN MAY BE FULLY ONE WITH GOD

John 17:22 says, "And the glory which You have given Me I have given to them, that they may be one, even as We are one." The Lord was saying, "Just as in You I am glorified along with Yourself, so I pray that in You they also will be glorified with You. Just as You desire that in You I have Your nature and be with You, so I pray that in You they also will have Your nature and be with You." Only in such a condition can all the believers be one as the Triune God is one.

Verses 23 and 24a say, "I in them, and You in Me, that they may be perfected into one, that the world may know that You have sent Me and have loved them even as You have loved Me. Father, concerning that which You have given Me, I desire that they also may be with Me where I am, that they may behold My glory, which You have given Me." I would like to ask you brothers and sisters what the Lord meant when He said, "Concerning that which You have given Me, I desire that they also may be with Me where I am, that they may behold My glory, which You have given Me." I believe that by now you surely understand. What the Lord meant was that He was now in the Father and He also would like His disciples to be with Him in the Father.

Therefore, what the Lord spoke in chapter fourteen is fully fulfilled. In chapter fourteen the Lord said, "In My Father's house are many abodes...for I go to prepare a place for you. And if I go and prepare a place for you, I am coming again and will receive you to Myself, so that where I am you also may be" (vv. 2-3). Now it is clear that this *where* does not at all refer to heaven, a place, but refers to being in God, that is, to being in the Father.

I repeat, what the Lord accomplished in His incarnation was only to bring God into man. He still had to go through death and resurrection to bring man into God. In His incarnation He only caused God to be made lowly. If He did not go through death and resurrection, He could not cause man to be glorified. His incarnation was for man to see how He lowered Himself as a man. His death and resurrection was to bring those who believe in Him into God that they may see the glory with which He is glorified in the Father and that they may be glorified along with Him and God.

Therefore, the Lord prayed, "Father, concerning that which You have given Me, I desire that they also may be with Me where I am, that they may behold My glory, which You have given Me." What is this glory? This glory is to be with God and to express God, that is, to be in God. The Lord seemed to be saying, "I was in You and I was with You. Now they have beheld how I became the Son of Man and how I lived as a lowly man, but they do not see how I am One who is in God and how I am glorified along with God. So now I ask You to bring them into You even as I am in You. In this way they can behold how I enjoy the glory with You." This was what the Lord meant, and this was what the Lord would accomplish in His death and resurrection. Through His death and resurrection He brought us into God just as He was in God. The more we learn to live in God, the more we know the glory of the Lord.

Verse 24 concludes, "For You loved Me before the foundation of the world." This means, "In eternity You loved Me and glorified Me along with You and in You."

Verses 25 and 26 say, "Righteous Father, though the world has not known You, yet I have known You, and these have known that You have sent Me. And I have made Your name known to them and will yet make it known, that the love with which You have loved Me may be in them, and I in them." This portion seems to be saying, "Just as You have loved Me and caused Me to be in You, to be one with You, and to enjoy the glory with You, so You will also love them and cause them to enter into You to be one with You and to enjoy the glory with You." This is what was meant by, "That the love with which You have loved Me may be in them."

THE CENTRAL THOUGHT
OF THE LORD'S LAST MESSAGE AND PRAYER
BEING THE ONENESS AND MUTUAL ABODE
OF GOD AND MAN

We have finished reading John 14, 15, 16, and 17. I will now pause briefly and ask the brothers and sisters to consider: In these four chapters, is the emphasis on the Lord's bringing us, the saved ones, from earth to heaven? Is there such a thought? In these four chapters can you recognize such a concept that the Lord's intention is to save us who are on the earth and bring us to heaven? The answer clearly is no. These four chapters concern the Lord's going through death and resurrection to save us who are outside of God into God, that is, to save us, who had absolutely nothing to do with God, to a point that not only do we have a relationship with God, but we even enter into God. I say again that His incarnation was to bring God into man. When He was incarnated, there was at that point one person on the earth who had God in Him. But if He had not gone through death and resurrection, man could not be in God, for man had not yet entered into God. Therefore, before John 14 you cannot find any verses in which the Lord told the disciples, "You are in Me" or "I am in you." You can at most find verses saying that the Lord was among the disciples. It is only after He said, "And if I go and prepare a place for you, I am coming again and will receive you to Myself" (14:3) that He could say, "You are in Me" and "I am in you." Do not forget 14:20, which says, "In that day you will know that I am in My Father, and you in Me, and I in you."

I hope the young brothers and sisters can take the time to

count how many *in*s there are in John 14, 15, 16, and 17. Just in the last sentence in the concluding prayer in John 17, "That the love with which You have loved Me may be in them, and I in them," there are two *in*s. You need to see that the central thought of the Lord's message and His concluding prayer is that a group of people who belong to Him—whom God chose before the foundation of the world, whom God set apart from the world, whom God would use to build His dwelling place—were outside of God and alienated from God, and they had not entered into God to be built with God. Therefore, He had to die on the cross and thereby deal with their sins, their flesh, their enemy, and the world within them so that He could open a way for them to enter into God and live in God. This is what is meant by His going to prepare a place for them. When He had prepared the place in such a way, He would come again, which is to resurrect and come not only to be among them but also to enter into them that they might receive the life of God. In this way He would bring them into God to be joined to God as one. Then they would receive the eternal life of God, know who God is, receive God's word, and thereby be separated from the world. Moreover, they would fully live in God, enjoy God's glory, and become one entity with God. This is the temple that the Lord built up after He resurrected and ascended to heaven. This temple is built with the resurrection life in His resurrection.

THE LORD NOT LEAVING AFTER HIS RESURRECTION BUT ABIDING IN THE BELIEVERS FOREVER

After John 17, chapter eighteen talks about the Lord's being betrayed and judged. Then chapter nineteen talks about His crucifixion for the accomplishing of redemption. In particular, it says that blood and water came out of the Lord's side (v. 34). Of the four Gospels, only John mentions blood and water. You need to realize that the coming out of blood and water was the Lord's preparing a place for the disciples. Blood is for redemption, and water is for imparting life. His death, on the one hand, was the shedding of blood for redemption, thus solving the problems we have before God. On the other hand, it was the releasing of the life of God that we may enter into God and have a union with God.

Then in chapter twenty He resurrected. We will read only a few verses, beginning with verse 19: "When therefore it was evening on that day, the first day of the week, and while the doors were shut where the disciples were for fear of the Jews, Jesus came and stood in the midst." Please keep in mind that this was His coming. In chapter fourteen He said that He was going; here in chapter twenty He came. He said, "Yet a little while and the world beholds Me no longer, but you behold Me" (14:19). The "little while" was three days according to the Jewish way of counting days, although it was only less than two days in another way of reckoning. The Lord came again into their midst and showed Himself to them. Verses 19b and 20 of chapter twenty continue, "And said to them, Peace be to you. And when He had said this, He showed them His hands and His side. The disciples therefore rejoiced at seeing the Lord." This proves that He was not merely a soul or a spirit but an actual man. This also fulfilled the word in John 16:22: "But I will see you again and your heart will rejoice."

Then Jesus said to them, "Peace be to you; as the Father has sent Me, I also send you" (20:21). This meant, "Just as the Father has sent Me, being within Me, so I also send you, being within you. I am in the Father and the Father is in Me. The words that I say to you I do not speak from Myself, but the Father who abides in Me speaks His words [14:10]. Now in the same way I also send you from within you and speak My words in you."

Verses 22 and 23 of chapter twenty continue, "And when He had said this, He breathed into them and said to them, Receive the Holy Spirit. Whosoever sins you forgive, they are forgiven them; and whosoever sins you retain, they are retained." Please keep in mind that the breath the Lord breathed into the disciples was an extraordinary breath. This breath was His transfiguration. He Himself was in that breath. "Receive the Holy Spirit" means "Receive Me. I am now entering into you just as this breath is entering into you. Previously I was in the flesh; I could only be in your midst. Now I can enter into you because I have been transfigured into the Spirit. From now on, I am no longer outside of you but inside of you. Therefore, whosoever sins you forgive, they are forgiven them; and whosoever sins you retain, they are retained. This is because it is not you who do this work, but it is I who do it. The only reason you have such great authority to forgive and retain the sins of others is that I am in you. You speak these words not by yourself, but it is I who speak My words in you."

Brothers and sisters, from then on the Lord was not only in the midst of the disciples but also in the disciples. His being in the disciples was invisible but very practical. I would like to ask you, did the Lord Jesus go away after verse 23? According to our concept, there should be an additional sentence in verse 23, saying, "After Jesus spoke this word He went away." However, there is not such a word in the Bible.

Verses 24 through 26 say, "But Thomas, one of the twelve, called Didymus, was not with them when Jesus came. The other disciples therefore said to him, We have seen the Lord! But he said to them, Unless I see in His hands the mark of the nails and put my finger into the mark of the nails and put my hand into His side, I will by no means believe. And after eight days, His disciples were again within, and Thomas was with them. Jesus came, though the doors were shut, and stood in the midst and said, Peace be to you." Please tell me what the story behind the Lord's coming is. To be precise, the Lord's coming here is not His coming but His appearing. He never left after He came on the previous Lord's Day evening. This is because when the Lord breathed into the disciples and said, "Receive the Holy Spirit," He entered into them and remained within them always; He never left at all.

Verses 27 through 29 continue, "Then He said to Thomas, Bring your finger here and see My hands, and bring your hand and put it into My side; and do not be unbelieving, but believing. Thomas answered and said to Him, My Lord and my God! Jesus said to him, Because you have seen Me, you have believed. Blessed are those who have not seen and have believed." Does the Bible then say, "After Jesus spoke these words, He went away"? No. John mentions only the Lord's coming, not His leaving.

After chapter twenty, there is still another chapter—chapter twenty-one. Without John 21 we may still think that the Lord went away. However, this chapter shows us that the Lord was still here. Let us read verses 1 through 7a. Verse 1 begins, "After these things Jesus manifested Himself again to the disciples at the Sea of Tiberias." It was not a matter of coming but a matter of being manifested. He never went, so He did not need to come. Rather, He lived in them. Verses 1b-4 say, "And He manifested Himself in this way: Simon Peter and Thomas, called Didymus, and Nathanael from Cana of Galilee and the sons of Zebedee and two others of His disciples were there together. Simon Peter said to them, I am going fishing. They said to him, We also are coming with you. They went forth and got into the boat, and that night they caught nothing. Now as soon as the morning broke, Jesus stood on the shore; however the disciples did not know that it was Jesus." They also had no idea how He came. Verses 5-7a continue, "Then Jesus said to them, Little children, you do not have any fish to eat, do you? They answered Him, No. And He said to them, Cast the net on the right side of the boat, and you will find some. They cast therefore, and they were no longer able to haul it in because of the abundance of fish. Then that disciple whom Jesus loved said to Peter, It is the Lord!" At this time they finally realized that it was the Lord. They did not realize it was the Lord until they saw so many fish. This is similar to what happened with the two disciples on their way to Emmaus (Luke 24); the Lord was in their midst, but they did not know it.

You can read through to the end of John 21, but you will not find that Jesus left them, that Jesus went away. It seems that the Gospel of John does not have a conclusion. John finished his writing, but there was no conclusion to it. In John 20 and 21 he uses two or three examples to show us that after the Lord's resurrection, He as the Spirit had entered into the disciples to be with them forever, never to leave. At times, due to their weaknesses, He would manifest Himself for them to see. That was not His coming but His manifestation. After His manifestation, He was hidden again. The Lord was still with them; He never left them.

Please keep in mind that this is the work accomplished

through the Lord's death and resurrection. He brings those who belong to Him fully into God, and as the Spirit He Himself abides in them that they may be fully built up together with God and become one with God. This is the temple He raised up. He seemed to say, "Destroy this temple which I obtained in My incarnation, and I will raise it up again in three days. I will resurrect from death and raise it up in resurrection with the resurrection life. I am now living in the body of one man, but after My resurrection I will live in the Body with millions of people." From our perspective as human beings living in time, today He is still building this temple in resurrection. From God's perspective, however, He has already resurrected and completed this temple, because with Him there is no element of time.

Dear brothers and sisters, this is the Gospel of John. Do not forget that the subject of the Gospel of John is the Word becoming flesh and tabernacling among us. That was a temporary temple; that was a single man. Men destroyed this temple, but the Lord raised it up in resurrection. His death and resurrection were to bring man into God that man might have a union with God. Now He abides in man, and man becomes a temple built by God.

CHAPTER FIVE

THE TURN CONCERNING
THE BUILDING OF GOD IN THE BIBLE

Scripture Reading: John 3:29; Rev. 21:2-3, 9-10; 19:7-9; Heb. 11:9-10, 13-16, 39-40; 12:18-19, 22-24

The last passage in the Scripture reading above, Hebrews 12:22-24, was poorly translated in the Chinese version of the Bible. A more appropriate translation should be, "But you have come forward to Mount Zion and to the city of the living God, the heavenly Jerusalem; and to myriads of angels, to the universal gathering; and to the church of the firstborn, who have been enrolled in the heavens; and to God, the Judge of all; and to the spirits of righteous men who have been made perfect; and to Jesus, the Mediator of a new covenant; and to the blood of sprinkling, which speaks something better than that of Abel." Eight items are mentioned here, joined by the same conjunction. First, there is Mount Zion; second, the city of the living God, the heavenly Jerusalem; third, the myriads of angels, the universal gathering; fourth, the church of the firstborn, who have been enrolled in the heavens; fifth, God, the Judge of all; sixth, the spirits of righteous men who have been made perfect; seventh, Jesus, the Mediator of a new covenant; and eighth, His sprinkled blood. These eight items are joined by seven *and*s.

Let me explain a little about these eight items. The first item is Mount Zion. We know that this Mount Zion does not denote the Mount Zion in the city of Jerusalem on earth. Rather, it denotes the Mount Zion in the heavens. The writer of the Epistle to the Hebrews was saying, "You have come forward to Mount Zion in the heavens." Please consider: Where were the recipients of this Epistle—on earth or in heaven?

Obviously they were still on earth. However, the writer of the Epistle was saying, "Although you are on the earth now, you have come forward to Mount Zion in the heavens." This passage of Scripture does not say that believers will go to heaven in the future. If this passage spoke about the believers' going to heaven, then they had already gone to heaven before they died, since the writer of the Epistle said, "You have come forward to Mount Zion." He was referring not to the Hebrew saints who were dead but to the saints who were alive and were reading this Epistle. Therefore, we are clear that this passage does not concern the believers' going to heaven after their death.

Then what is the meaning of Mount Zion here? We know that the book of Hebrews was written at that time to the Hebrew believers, the Jews. The background of the Jews was the Old Testament. One day, when Moses led the children of Israel to Mount Sinai, God descended upon it. The mountain was set on fire, and there were darkness, gloom, a whirlwind, the sound of a trumpet, and the voice of words. None of the children of Israel could bear that dreadful situation (Exo. 19:11-18). Today, however, in the New Testament age, we are no longer under the condemnation of the law but under the grace of the new covenant. Therefore, the author of the book of Hebrews seemed to be saying, "Today because you believe in the Lord, you have not come to such a place as Mount Sinai to inherit the law, but you have come to Mount Zion in the new covenant to receive grace."

The second item is the city of the living God, the heavenly Jerusalem. In addition, there are the myriads of angels, the universal gathering, and the church of the firstborn. These firstborn ones have not gone up to the heavens, but they have already been enrolled in the heavens. These are the New Testament saints. Besides these, there are God Himself and the spirits of righteous men who have been made perfect. The righteous men who have been made perfect obviously were the saved ones in the Old Testament. However, these saved ones did not belong to the old covenant but to the new covenant. Why is this? It is because, although they lived in the Old Testament age, they still belonged to God's eternal covenant, the covenant God made with Abraham. The covenant God made with Abraham was a covenant of grace and an eternal covenant. Later, because the children of Israel did not know the covenant and rejected that covenant, God enacted on Mount Sinai another covenant, the covenant of law, which is the old covenant. Under this covenant, there is only Mount Sinai with thunder, lightning, fire, the sound of a trumpet, and the voice of the words of God. Under this covenant, no one can be saved.

The old covenant we often speak of denotes not only the old covenant under the law; sometimes it also denotes the entire age of the Old Testament. According to the old covenant of the law, there were certainly no saved ones, but according to the entire age of the Old Testament, there were still many saved ones. For example, Abraham, Isaac, and Jacob were all people in the age of the Old Testament, but they were all saved. However, they were not saved under the old covenant of the law. They did not belong to the old covenant of the law but to the eternal covenant God made with Abraham.

Please remember that the new covenant is the continuation of the covenant God made with Abraham. This matter is clearly explained in Galatians 3 and 4. Originally, there was the covenant of Abraham. Then the covenant of law was added, and following this, the new covenant. The covenant of law inserted in between was temporary. In time God recovered the covenant of Abraham, which became the new covenant. Therefore, there are saved ones only under the covenant of Abraham and the new covenant; there are no saved ones under the covenant of law. Under the covenant of law, what men saw was Mount Sinai. This mountain had fire, darkness, gloom, a whirlwind, the sound of a trumpet, and a terrible voice. Yet in the covenant of grace, including the covenant of Abraham and the new covenant, there are Mount Zion in the heavens, the city of the living God, the angels, the church, the God who judges all, the spirits of those who were saved under the covenant of Abraham in the Old Testament age, Jesus the Mediator of a new covenant, and His sprinkled blood. These are all matters of the new covenant.

The author of the book of Hebrews mentions these eight items here for us to see that today we have not come to Mount

Sinai of the old covenant law, but we have come to Mount Zion of the new covenant grace. He is not talking about going to heaven at all. Therefore, it is incorrect to suppose that this passage concerns the believers' going to heaven. I say again that if this refers to going to heaven, then those who read the Epistle had already left the earth and gone up to heaven before they died. I believe these words are clear enough.

This is a little bit of biblical exposition. I hope that you would not see expounding the Bible as something simple. Gradually you will see that expounding the Bible is a great matter, not simple at all.

A GREAT TURN IN THE BIBLE

In this message we will make a great turn. We have just turned from the covenant of Abraham to the covenant of law, and again from the covenant of law to the new covenant, showing that the new covenant is the continuation of the covenant of Abraham. That was only a small turn. Now we will make a great turn. I would like to make it as simple as possible, so I will speak on it point by point.

The first point is that the Lord became flesh and tabernacled among us. The Lord in the flesh was a tabernacle. From God's point of view, the Lord's incarnation was His coming to the earth to set up a tabernacle for Him to have a dwelling place.

Second, for what purpose did the incarnated Lord come to the earth? The Bible says that He came to be the Bridegroom to marry His bride. The Gospel of John shows us that when John the Baptist was on earth, his disciples saw that many who were following him turned to follow the Lord Jesus, so they became resentful and went and told him. He then said, "He who has the bride is the bridegroom" (John 3:29a). His meaning was, "I am not the bridegroom. I do not have the bride. He has the bride. It is right for people to follow Him; they should not follow me. I am just the friend of the bridegroom. I stand here, and seeing Him, I rejoice" (vv. 26-29). We know that John the Baptist testified twice for the Lord Jesus. One time he said, "Behold, the Lamb of God, who takes away the sin of the world!" (1:29). The other time he said, "He who has the bride is the bridegroom." The Lord became flesh and tabernacled among us, and this One was the Bridegroom who came for the bride.

Who is the bride, and when will the Lord marry the bride? For this we need to go to Revelation. John wrote not only the Gospel of John and the Epistles of John; he also wrote Revelation. If you cannot find the answers after you have read his Gospel and his Epistles, you can still read his Revelation. You find a little hint when you come to Revelation 19. Here we find the declaration: "The marriage of the Lamb has come" (v. 7). This is a story of marriage—the Lamb is getting married. In the beginning of his Gospel, John speaks of the Lamb and the Bridegroom, and now in Revelation he says that the marriage of the Lamb has come. This means that the Lamb as the Bridegroom is marrying the bride.

Whom is He marrying? Revelation 19 says that the bride is clothed in fine linen, bright and clean, which is the righteousnesses of the saints (v. 8). From this you can understand that the bride He is marrying is composed of the saints redeemed by God. This is still not clear enough. When you come to chapter twenty-one, you see that it says, "I saw the holy city, New Jerusalem, coming down out of heaven from God, prepared as a bride adorned for her husband" (v. 2). Then it says that the city which came down out of heaven is the tabernacle of God with men (v. 3). So you see that the bride, the wife, of the Lamb is a city. The New Jerusalem is the bride, the wife, of the Lamb.

Brothers and sisters, who is the bride? On the one hand, since the bride is a city, she is a corporate person composed of all the saved ones, the saints. On the other hand, this bride is also the tabernacle God built among men, which in principle is the same as the tabernacle God pitched in His incarnation. Please pay attention to the turn here. It is not merely a turn but a circular three-hundred-sixty-degree turn, from pitching a tabernacle to pitching a tabernacle. God became a man and tabernacled among men. This tabernacling God is the Bridegroom, and the bride He is marrying is a composition of the saved ones. This bride is also a city, and this city is the tabernacle God pitched among men.

Since it is a city coming down out of heaven, the city of New Jerusalem, the bride, is heavenly. Hebrews 11 and 12 also speak of this city. Chapter eleven says that in the Old Testament times, those to whom the promise was made, such as Abraham, Isaac, and Jacob, all longed after this city (v. 16). Why did they long after this city? It is because they felt that they were strangers on the earth, wanderers without a home. Even though in his lifetime Abraham did have a place to live on the earth, and so did Isaac and Jacob, according to their feeling they were only strangers and sojourners on the earth; the earth was not their own country. Therefore, they eagerly waited for the city which has the foundations. I do not know whether Abraham, Isaac, or Jacob realized what that city was, but the Holy Spirit made them feel that they had no dwelling place on earth and that the earth was not their own country. They were strangers on the earth, so they longed after a heavenly country, which is the city whose Architect and Builder is God.

Now I would like to ask you brothers and sisters, "What exactly is the city that Abraham, Isaac, and Jacob longed after?" At their time they might not have been clear. They simply felt that the earth was not their dwelling place but merely a place where they wandered and sojourned. Therefore, they longed after an eternal country, a heavenly one, whose Architect and Builder is God. However, today we are the saints of the New Testament age and we have been instructed. Therefore, we should be much clearer than they were. Today we know that the city they longed after is the city of New Jerusalem.

What then is the city of New Jerusalem? It is the bride, the wife, of the Lamb. What is the bride, the wife, of the Lamb? She is a group of people redeemed by the Lord, a group of people who are mingled with God as one to become God's tabernacle. What is this tabernacle? It is the very God who tabernacled among men by putting on humanity, entering into humanity, and being mingled with humanity. This is the country that Abraham, Isaac, and Jacob longed after, which is also their eternal dwelling place. In one sense, Abraham, Isaac, and Jacob have not entered into it, because Hebrews 11 clearly says, "And these all, having obtained a good testimony through their faith, did not obtain the promise, because God has provided something better for us [that is, for those who are saved in the New Testament age], so that apart from us they [that is, those who were saved in the Old Testament age] would not be made perfect" (vv. 39-40). These are all descriptions of a spiritual mystery which we cannot fully comprehend with our mind at this time.

The end of Revelation says that the time has come; that is, the bride, the holy city, has come. The bride includes all those who were saved in the Old Testament and all those who are saved in the New Testament. This is indicated by the gates and walls of the New Jerusalem being inscribed with the names of the twelve New Testament apostles, which represent those who are saved in the New Testament age, and the names of the twelve tribes, which represent those who were saved in the Old Testament age (21:12, 14). Therefore, this city is a composition of those who are saved in the two ages—the Old Testament age and the New Testament age. This city is the bride, the wife, of the Lamb. Even today God still has not yet completed this city; He is still building it.

We have made a great turn here. I hope that you brothers and sisters remember this great turn. This great turn links the entire Gospel of John, Revelation, and Hebrews 11 and 12.

THE BUILDING WORK OF GOD BEING ONE

Now we would raise another question. God first created, and after creation He builds. We now understand a little about what God wants to build. The Bible seems to present two aspects concerning the building of God. On the one hand, God is building the church. The Lord Jesus said, "Upon this rock I will build My church" (Matt. 16:18). The apostle Paul said that today God is building the Body of Christ, which is the church. Peter said that we come to the Lord as living stones, being built up as a spiritual house. They all spoke about God building the church. On the other hand, the Bible says that God is building a city. The city Abraham longed after is promised by God, and it is also designed and built by God.

Now let me ask you a question. Does this mean that God

has two buildings in the universe? Does it mean that God is building the church on earth, on the one hand, and building the holy city in the heavens, on the other? Bible expositors throughout the ages all seem to have this view, including Darby. They say that Matthew 16 is on the building of the church and Ephesians 2 and 4 are also on the building of the church. First Corinthians 3 says, "You are...God's building" (v. 9); this also concerns the building of the church. First Peter 2 contains words referring to the building of the church. Even 1 Corinthians 14 frequently refers to the building of the church. On the other hand, the expositors say that Hebrews 11 speaks about God's building of the holy city, and that John 14, in which the Lord said, "I go and prepare a place for you," also refers to His building of the holy city. Therefore, it seems that the Bible expositors throughout the ages have divided God's work of building into two—one that He is building the church on the earth, and the other that He is building the holy city in the heavens.

Brothers and sisters, do you think there are two buildings or one? If there were two, then there would be many problems. If today God is building the church on the earth, and at the same time He is building the holy city in the heavens, then at the end when both are finished, which one will God want? Can it be that in eternity there will be a holy city as well as a church? We know that there will be only one holy city in eternity. Therefore, we can boldly conclude that today God does not have two buildings; He has only one. God's building of the holy city is His building of the church, and God's building of the church is His building of the holy city.

This is very clear in the Bible because when we read to the end of the Bible, we see that the holy city includes the church. It says there that in the holy city are the names of the twelve apostles, who represent the church. It also says that the holy city is the tabernacle of God with men. The tabernacle is the precursor to the temple, and the church is the temple of God. Therefore, when the holy city is manifested, there is no temple in it, for the city is the very temple; it is the enlargement of the temple. These all show us that God has only one building in the universe. He does not have two buildings. It is not as some Bible expositors say, that God, on the one hand, is building the church in the believers through His life, and on the other hand, He is building a city in the heavens with gold, pearl, and precious stones. The Bible never says this.

I would like for all the brothers and sisters to see that God does not have a second building. In the entire universe, God has only one building. This building work of God is His building Himself into man and building man into Himself. This is His mingling together with man to become the mutual habitation of God and man. From Genesis 2, after God completed His creation, He placed Himself before man to be man's bread of life for man to take in. Since then God has been doing a building work on man and in man. Although later Satan came in to interfere, God never abandoned this goal.

Therefore, in the Old Testament you also see many instances where God came to man to be joined to man. He charged the Israelites to build a tabernacle for Him. Then when the Israelites entered Canaan, He told them to build a temple. These signify that He wants to dwell among His people, having His people as His dwelling place. I have said again and again that all the stories of the Old Testament, from the beginning to the end, are stories of the tabernacle and the temple. The entire Old Testament is centered on the tabernacle and the temple. Even when the temple was destroyed, the central subject of the subsequent prophecies was still to have the children of Israel return and rebuild the temple.

What was the story of the temple? The story of the temple was God's mingling together with those who were saved in the Old Testament age to become a house, the dwelling place of God and also the abode of those who belonged to God.

In the New Testament God became flesh and entered into humanity. The Bible says that this was God's tabernacling among men. It also says that the flesh the Lord became was a temple. Those who know the Bible understand that this is an extension to the Old Testament story. The flesh the Lord put on was signified by the tabernacle among the Israelites in the Old Testament and also the temple in the land of Canaan. The Lord said, "Destroy this temple, and in three days I will raise it up" (John 2:19). We all know that this refers to the

Lord's resurrection. Therefore, the Lord's incarnation was for the building of the temple, and the Lord's death and resurrection were also for the building of the temple.

For this reason in Matthew 16 the Lord said, "Upon this rock I will build My church" (v. 18). This rock refers to the resurrected Christ. It is written in the Bible that from the time of the Lord's resurrection, He has been doing this building work as the Spirit. He gave some as apostles, some as prophets, some as evangelists, and some as shepherds and teachers, and their work is for the building of the church (Eph. 4:11-12). Therefore, the goal of the apostles' work is not merely to save sinners or to edify the saints but to save sinners as materials for the building of the dwelling place of God and to edify and perfect the saints with the purpose that the saints might be built into this building of God. All of their work, be it preaching the gospel or edifying the saints, takes the building of this spiritual house as the goal.

This is different from the work of many who preach the word today. Some of them take saving sinners as their aim, and some take edifying saints as their goal. The apostles, however, were not like this. While they did save sinners, saving sinners was not their purpose. While they did edify saints, they did not consider that as their goal. All of their work took the building of God's spiritual house as the purpose and the building of God's dwelling place as the goal. The apostle Paul said that as a wise master builder he had laid the foundation—Jesus Christ—and another built upon it, but that each man ought to take heed how he builds upon it—with gold, silver, and precious stones or with wood, grass, and stubble (1 Cor. 3:10-12). He said that the Corinthians were God's building and that they, the apostles, were God's fellow workers who were building up the Corinthians (v. 9). He also said, "If anyone destroys the temple of God, God will destroy him" (v. 17). Here the temple refers to the church, not man's body. If anyone destroys the temple of God, which is the church, God will destroy him, because this is the temple that He has been building throughout the generations. Brothers and sisters, we also are God's fellow workers, and our goal also should be the building of God.

The church today is God's temple, God's house, and when it is built, it becomes the city. The city is the enlargement of the house. This city includes the house in the Old Testament and also the house in the New Testament. The story of the Old Testament is the temple, and the story of the New Testament is the church. The work God did in the Old Testament was to build His people, the Israelites, that they might become the house of God. Every work God does in the New Testament is still to build the saints that they may be the house of God. The house in the Old Testament is the temple, while the house in the New Testament is the church. The entire Old Testament is centered on the temple; the entire New Testament is centered on the church. When both are completed, the work that God has been doing throughout the ages will be aggregated to become a city. That is why both the names of the twelve tribes and the names of the twelve apostles are in the city. The names of the twelve apostles represent the church, the house in the New Testament, while the names of the twelve tribes represent the Israelites, the house of Israel in the Old Testament. The two houses of the Old Testament and New Testament join together to become a city. This city is the eternal abode of God and His redeemed people. It is also the bride that God as the Bridegroom marries. God wants to be fully united, to become one, with her. Hence, this city is the tabernacle He built among men as His eternal dwelling place and also as the eternal abode of all of us who are saved.

Brothers and sisters, we need to see that the work that God has been doing among His people throughout the generations is this building work. We who are saved are the materials in this building. The edification we receive after we are saved is not for us to become items for exhibition but to become materials for building. In the past you were natural and wild and could not be coordinated and built together with others. But now due to the work of grace in you, you have been dealt with, broken, perfected, and made fit for God's building. Brothers and sisters, this is the work God wants to do among us today. Only this can bring in God's blessing. Only by this can we touch the presence of God and satisfy God's heart's desire.

We should not hope to be built up in the future. We should believe that God is doing this building work in us today. For six thousand years this building work is what God has been doing, and it is also what Satan has been undermining. As Satan damaged and destroyed the temple in the Old Testament, in the same way he is using various stratagems to damage and destroy the church in the New Testament. The work of Satan is to damage and destroy the building of God. We can almost say that Satan would allow people to do any kind of work, but he would never allow people to build the church. Whenever you bring up the matter of the building of the church, you encounter Satan's opposition, attack, and damage. This is because the one thing Satan hates the most is God's building work, God's central work, in the universe.

CHAPTER SIX

THE PLACE WHERE THE BELIEVERS GO

A GENERAL INACCURATE BELIEF

We will begin by studying some Scriptures to help everyone to know the truth concerning the place where the believers go. In these days we have mentioned God's building, especially the abode of God with the believers. Because of this, we would like to address the inaccurate belief in Christianity concerning the matter of going to a heavenly mansion. The concept of going to a heavenly mansion is very strong in Roman Catholicism, even to the extent that it has become a superstition in an extreme. Even in Protestantism, the poison of this superstition of Catholicism is still not altogether removed. Up to this day, among the many children of God there still exists this kind of inaccurate concept concerning going to a heavenly mansion. Therefore, I feel that we should come together to study the Word concerning this matter.

Before we study the Bible, I would like to speak a little word concerning the general belief in Christianity. I believe that the brothers and sisters all know that among orthodox Christians it is universally believed that when a person who believes in the Lord and is saved dies, although his body is left on the earth, his spirit goes to a heavenly mansion, to the place where God and the Lord Jesus are. Therefore, at a Christian's funeral the pastor or preacher usually says something like this: "Do not be troubled or sorrowful. This person has been taken by the Lord. He has gone to a heavenly mansion and is in God's house enjoying the eternal blessing with God. That place has gates of pearl, walls of jasper, and streets of gold. It is far better than anywhere else. Therefore, we should be happy and rejoice for him. One day we also will take this way and go to that beautiful place."

Naturally, everyone who hears such a message with candied words will have a sweet sensation. However, we know that deceiving words almost always are very pleasant to our ears. In the previous year when I was overseas, I read some notes of a message spoken by a pastor at the funeral of an aged woman. He said over and over again that this aged woman has gone now to a heavenly mansion. While I was reading it, I said in my heart, "This is nonsense. This is altogether cheating people. Fortunately, this old woman cannot come back. If she could, she would tell you, 'This is altogether false. I am not in a heavenly mansion. Where I am, you do not know.'" It seems that I am speaking sarcastically. But I want the brothers and sisters to have a deep impression that today in Christianity the teaching concerning going to a heavenly mansion is inaccurate.

THE REVELATION OF THE HOLY SCRIPTURES

Now we want to see where the spirit and soul of a saved person go if he dies before the Lord's coming. We must study this matter clearly and not merely listen to the traditional teaching in Christianity. I have said many times that Christianity has brought in many things that are wrong and we must therefore exercise our discernment. We want the gospel, we want the Bible, and we want the Lord Himself, but we do not want Christianity with its organization and doctrines. We abandon the traditional theology in Christianity with all its errors.

Now we come to see what the Bible says concerning this matter. First let us read Luke 16:22: "And the beggar died, and he was carried away by the angels into Abraham's bosom." We all have to admit that this beggar Lazarus was a saved one. He would not have been carried away by the angels into Abraham's bosom unless he was a saved one. Now we must ask, What kind of place is Abraham's bosom? Once the bosom is mentioned, we know it means comfort. We all know that the mother's bosom is a place where a child is most comforted. Verse 25 says, "Abraham said...now he is comforted here."

Hence, Abraham's bosom is a place of comfort and not a place of anguish.

Let us go back and read from the second half of verse 22 through verse 23: "And the rich man also died and was buried. And in Hades he lifted up his eyes, being in torment, and saw Abraham from afar and Lazarus in his bosom." Here it clearly says that the rich man died, his body was buried, and his spirit went down to Hades. Furthermore, he lifted up his eyes and saw Abraham from afar, and he also saw Lazarus in Abraham's bosom.

Let us go on and read verses 24 through 26: "And he called out and said, Father Abraham, have mercy on me and send Lazarus to dip the tip of his finger in water and cool my tongue, because I am in anguish in this flame. But Abraham said, Child, remember that in your lifetime you fully received your good things, and Lazarus likewise bad things; but now he is comforted here, and you are in anguish. And besides all these things, between us and you a great chasm is fixed, so that those wanting to pass from here to you cannot, neither from there to us may any cross over." Here it says that Lazarus was being comforted in Abraham's bosom, but the rich man was suffering anguish in Hades. The rich man in Hades saw from afar Lazarus in Abraham's bosom. This shows that they were separated by quite a distance from each another, and not only so, there was a great chasm fixed between them so that they could not pass one to the other. We know that the rich man was in Hades. Now we need to ask where Lazarus and Abraham were.

We should come to the Word to find the answer. Genesis 25:8 says, "And Abraham expired and died in a good old age, an old man and full of days, and he was gathered to his people." Verses 34 and 35 of chapter thirty-seven say, "And Jacob tore his garments and put sackcloth upon his loins and mourned for his son many days. And all his sons and all his daughters rose up to comfort him; but he refused to be comforted and said, Surely I will go down to Sheol to my son, mourning." Then 42:38 says, "But he said, My son shall not go down with you, for his brother is dead, and he alone is left. And if harm should befall him on the way in which you go,

then you will bring down my gray hairs in sorrow to Sheol."
Finally, 47:29-30 says, "And the time for Israel to die drew
near. And he called his son Joseph and said to him...when I
lie down with my fathers." Jacob's grandfather was Abraham,
and Jacob's father was Isaac. Here, to "lie down with" means
to die. Jacob said that his death was his going down to Sheol.
He also said that the time of his death was the time when he
would lie down with his fathers. By this we are clear that the
spirits of Abraham, Isaac, Jacob, and the Old Testament
saints also went to Hades at their death.

You may be frightened at the mention of Hades and cry,
"Alas! How terrible it is for a person to die and go down to
Hades! Is it not equivalent to going to hell?" Please do not be
scared; it is not that simple. If we have the time, we can read
all the verses in the Old Testament concerning Hades; then
we will be clearer. Many places in the Old Testament plainly
tell us that Abraham, Isaac, Jacob, and all the saints who
received the promise went down to Hades (Sheol) after their
death.

In Luke 16 the Lord said that after Lazarus died, his spirit
was in the bosom of Abraham to be comforted. Therefore, he
was in a place where he was comforted. Although he went
down to Hades, the Hades where he was was different from
the "Hades" commonly known to people.

According to Luke 16, Hades is clearly divided into two
sections. Between these two sections a great chasm is fixed so
that those in one section cannot pass to the other, and vice
versa. One section is the section of torment, while the other is
the section of comfort. The section of torment is for the per-
ishing people of the world, whereas the section of comfort is
for saved saints. This is very clear.

Concerning Hades, I want to add another word. What is
Hades? Hades is the place where the disembodied spirits, the
spirits without a body, are kept. We must know that when a
human being leaves his body and becomes merely a spirit,
that is abnormal. The Bible says that this is like a person who
is naked, unclothed. We all are sitting in this meeting hall
today. If a brother were to walk in naked, would you let him
stand here? I believe we all would send him to a small room,

ask him to wait there for a while, give him some clothes, and tell him to come out after he had clothed himself. This is a small illustration. When a person dies, his spirit puts off his body. A person's body is his clothing; a spirit without a body is naked. Hence, when one dies and puts off his body, he becomes a disembodied spirit. This condition is very abnormal. Therefore, God has arranged a place for the dead ones to be kept until the time of their resurrection when they will put on their body. This waiting place is Hades. All dead persons, their bodies being left on earth and their spirits separated from their bodies and becoming naked, go to wait in Hades.

However, the spirits who are in Hades are divided into two groups. One group is composed of the saved ones, and the other group is composed of the perished ones. Therefore, Hades is divided into two sections, one for the perished spirits and the other for the saved spirits. Although it is divided into two sections, as a whole it is called Hades in the Bible. This is because whether they are saved spirits or unsaved spirits, they all are disembodied spirits; they are naked and should not be seen. Hence, they have to be put in a place where they will wait for the time of resurrection to be clothed with their body; everything will be resolved at that time. Therefore, Hades is divided into two sections, one section being a place of torment, and the other section being a place of comfort. Both sections are called Hades. We should not be frightened when we hear the mention of Hades, for there is more to it than we think.

Let us go on to read Luke 23:42, which is the word spoken by the saved thief who was crucified with the Lord: "Jesus, remember me when You come into Your kingdom." This thief did not know the truth, but because he heard that the Lord Jesus would be King and would receive a kingdom, he hoped that the Lord would remember him when He came into His kingdom. Although his prayer was very confused, the Lord's answer was very clear. Verse 43 says, "And He said to him, Truly I say to you, Today you shall be with Me in Paradise." Please notice that the Lord did not say, "After three days you will be with Me in Paradise." Rather, He said, "Today you shall be with Me in Paradise." This "today" was, of course, the very day of the Lord's crucifixion. Therefore, it is evident that Paradise is the place where the Lord went after His crucifixion and before His resurrection.

Matthew 12:40 says, "For just as Jonah was in the belly of the great fish three days and three nights, so will the Son of Man be in the heart of the earth three days and three nights." Now I want to ask you, is Paradise in the heavenly mansion? If you put these two portions of the Word together, you will know where Paradise is. Before He was crucified, the Lord told the saved thief, "Today you shall be with Me in Paradise." Then, from the first day to the third day after His death, the Lord was in the heart of the earth. Hence, this clearly shows us that Paradise is in the heart of the earth. Perhaps some will say that the Lord being three days and three nights in the heart of the earth refers to His body being buried in the earth. But no, the Greek text here is "the heart of the earth" and does not refer to the place just under the surface of the earth. Thus, it does not refer to the burial of His body.

We will read another passage, and then we will be clearer that after His death the Lord was in Hades for three days. Acts 2:24-32 says,

> Whom God has raised up, having loosed the pangs of death, since it was not possible for Him to be held by it. For David says regarding Him, "I saw the Lord continually before me, because He is on my right hand, that I may not be shaken. Therefore my heart was made glad and my tongue exulted; moreover, also my flesh will rest in hope [referring to being buried in the tomb full of hope, awaiting resurrection], because You will not abandon my soul to Hades, nor will You permit Your Holy One to see corruption. You have made known to me the ways of life; You will make me full of gladness with Your presence." Men, brothers, I can say to you plainly concerning the patriarch David that he both deceased and was buried, and his tomb is among us until this day. Therefore, being a prophet and knowing that God had sworn with an oath to him to seat One from the fruit of his loins upon his throne, he, seeing this before-

hand, spoke concerning the resurrection of the Christ, that neither was He abandoned to Hades, nor did His flesh see corruption. This Jesus God has raised up.

This word plainly tells us that after the Lord's death and before His resurrection, His body was buried in the earth, yet His spirit and soul went to Hades. "Today you shall be with Me in Paradise." "So will the Son of Man be in the heart of the earth three days and three nights." "You will not abandon my soul to Hades." When you put these three portions of the Word together, immediately you clearly see that the Paradise where the Lord went after His death is the heart of the earth in Hades. That Paradise is the place where Abraham is, the place in Hades where the saved ones are comforted. Although it is Hades, it is a place of comfort. Hence, it is Paradise.

Now we are clear that Abraham's bosom is in Paradise, and that Paradise is the pleasant section of Hades, the place where men are comforted after they die. This is acknowledged by orthodox Bible expositors in Christianity, and it is acknowledged even by some who say that the believers go to a heavenly mansion after they die. Certain ones say that the Old Testament saints, the saints who died before the resurrection of the Lord Jesus, went to Paradise in Hades, that even the Lord Jesus went there to stay for three days and three nights, and that the saved thief also went there. They say, however, that on the day of the resurrection of the Lord Jesus, this pleasant section—Paradise—was transferred to heaven by the Lord Jesus.

The Scofield Reference Bible says something to this effect. The footnote on Luke 16:23 separates Hades into two states—Hades before the ascension of Christ and Hades since the ascension of Christ. Before Christ's ascension, Hades had two sections occupied by the saved ones and the perished ones respectively, as we have said earlier. Up to the present time the unsaved dead persons are still suffering anguish in Hades, waiting for the coming of the final judgment. But, after the ascension of Christ, the spirits and souls of the saved ones were moved with the Lord Jesus from Paradise into heaven. Hence, Paradise is now in heaven where God is. The saved ones who die today in the church age depart from their body to be with the Lord. Hence, they are in Paradise in heaven.

Is this kind of interpretation accurate? Has Paradise been transferred? Has it been transferred from Hades to the third heaven? We need to study this matter. The main basis of those who say that Paradise has been transferred is Ephesians 4. Verse 8 says, "Having ascended to the height, He led captive those taken captive and gave gifts to men." Who are "those taken captive"? Are they not (some ask) the souls of the saved ones in the Old Testament age? They were captured and brought to Hades by Satan. They were redeemed and did not have to die, yet they were taken captive by Satan through death. Now the Lord Jesus has abolished death and destroyed the devil, the one who has the might of death, so when the Lord was resurrected from death, death no longer has power over these saints. These souls who had been taken captive by death were captured back by the Lord. Those who hold this kind of interpretation ask, "Since these souls have been led captive and come back, where should they be put?" No doubt, they say, they were brought by the Lord with Him to heaven.

This kind of interpretation is farfetched. Concerning the portion of the Word in Ephesians 4, there is great debate over the translation. The expositors who were experts in the Greek language told us the meaning here is that the Lord captured the enemy's capturing power. Satan, as one who always captures people, has the capturing power. We know that his capturing power is the power of death; death is the power of Satan by which he captures people. According to these expositors, at the time of the Lord's resurrection and ascension, Satan was disarmed of his power of death; his capturing power was stripped off and taken captive by the Lord. This is consistent with the thought of the Scriptures. However, regardless of which translation one uses, to merely use Ephesians 4 as the basis to say that Paradise has been transferred is truly farfetched.

Those who claim that Paradise has been transferred use 2 Corinthians 12 as their second basis. They say, "Does it not plainly tell us that Paradise is in the third heaven?" Now let us read 2 Corinthians 12, beginning with verse 1: "To boast is necessary, though indeed not expedient; yet I will come to visions and revelations of the Lord." Please remember that the subject of this chapter is neither Paradise nor a heavenly mansion but visions and revelations of the Lord. "I know a man in Christ, fourteen years ago (whether in the body I do not know, or outside the body I do not know; God knows) such a one was caught away to the third heaven. And I know such a man (whether in the body or outside the body, I do not know; God knows), that he was caught away into Paradise" (vv. 2-4). Those who hold the view that Paradise has been transferred strongly use this portion as their basis. They say, "If Paradise has not been transferred, how can it be in the third heaven? At the Lord's death Paradise was clearly in Hades, but the Paradise here is in the third heaven. Does this not show that Paradise has been transferred?" Verses 4 to 7 continue, "That he was caught away into Paradise and heard unspeakable words, which it is not allowed for a man to speak. On behalf of such a one I will boast, but on behalf of myself I will not boast, except in my weaknesses. For if I desire to boast, I will not be foolish, for I will speak the truth; but I refrain lest anyone account of me something above what he sees me to be or hears from me. And because of the transcendence of the revelations, in order that I might not be exceedingly lifted up, there was given to me a thorn in the flesh."

Before I go on to expound, I would like to ask a question: Why did the apostle twice say that he knew such a man, whether in the body or outside the body, he did not know, but God knew? Based on the Chinese translation it is hard to answer, but if you study the original text, right away you are clear. A very important word was omitted in the Chinese version—the conjunction *and* at the beginning of verse 3: "Such a one was caught away to the third heaven. *And* I know such a man...that he was caught away into Paradise." Here *was caught away* is also a big problem. The phrase may be translated "was caught up," or it may be translated "was caught away," as some English versions have. According to the context, it is clear that the translation which reads "was caught up to

Paradise" is barely acceptable, because to be caught up implies to go up from down below.

Furthermore, a number of versions put "whether in the body or outside the body, I do not know; God knows" in parenthesis, making it easier to read, since these words are merely for emphasis. Now let us read this portion again as follows: "I know a man in Christ, fourteen years ago...such a one was caught away to the third heaven. *And* I know such a man,...that he was caught away into Paradise." By reading it this way you can no longer insist that Paradise is in the third heaven. For example, I know that Brother Chang was sitting in the elders' room two hours ago, and I know that he is sitting in this meeting hall now. Can you say that this meeting hall is the elders' room? I believe the third heaven is the third heaven, and Paradise is Paradise. If Paradise and the third heaven are the same place, there is no need to use *and*. Since *and* is used, they must be two different places. This is a logical explanation based on the original text.

We have to know that here the apostle is not talking about Paradise being in the third heaven. Here he is talking about the revelations he received. The revelations God gave him were exceedingly great in that he was shown the situation of the entire universe. God showed the apostle Paul all the "stories" in the universe concerning God and man.

The stories of God and man in the universe occur in three places: in heaven, on earth, and under the earth. *In heaven* refers to the third heaven, *on earth*—this we all know, and *under the earth* refers to Hades, the place where the spirits of the dead persons are. All the stories of God and man in the universe occur in these three places. Philippians 2:9-11 says that when God exalts the Lord to the highest peak, those who are in heaven and on earth and under the earth will bow their knees, and all will openly confess that Jesus Christ is Lord. Therefore, there are three distinct places in the universe.

God gave the apostle Paul a great revelation that he might understand all the matters related to God and man. We should believe that Paul was very clear concerning the things on earth; hence, what God needed to show him were the things in the third heaven and the things in Paradise under the earth. God gave him a full revelation by bringing him to the third heaven to take a look there and then by bringing him to Paradise under the earth to take a look. Therefore, Paul said that he was caught away to the third heaven and he was also caught away into Paradise and heard unspeakable words. He was a man on earth, but he had been to heaven and he also had been to Paradise under the earth. Hence, the revelations that he received were truly exceedingly great. Therefore, what the apostle meant here is, "I am a person born on earth, yet I was caught away to heaven, and I also was caught away into Paradise, which is under the earth. I know the things on earth, I know the things in heaven, and I also know the things in Paradise under the earth. Therefore, the revelations that I received are exceedingly great." This shows us that Paradise is not in the third heaven. On the contrary, if you read this portion carefully, you can see that the third heaven is in heaven and Paradise is under the earth. Hence, after the Lord's ascension, Paradise was not transferred; it is still under the earth. (This Paradise is not the same as the Paradise mentioned in Revelation 2:7. This is the Paradise in Hades, whereas that one is the coming New Jerusalem, for in its midst is the tree of life.)

Let us go on to read Revelation 6:9-11: "And when He opened the fifth seal, I saw underneath the altar the souls of those who had been slain because of the word of God and because of the testimony which they had. And they cried with a loud voice, saying, How long, O Master, holy and true, will You not judge and avenge our blood on those who dwell on the earth? And to each of them was given a white robe; and it was said to them that they should rest yet a little while, until also the number of their fellow slaves and their brothers who were about to be killed, even as they were, is completed." This portion of the Word says that the souls of those who had been slain because of their testimony on behalf of the Lord, the souls of the Lord's martyrs, were underneath the altar. The altar is in the outer court of the tabernacle. All Bible students acknowledge that the tabernacle signifies the earth and the altar signifies the cross. The cross is not something placed in heaven; it is something on earth. Therefore, the souls under the altar are the souls under the earth. This shows us that at the time of Revelation 6, the souls of the Lord's martyrs are still under the altar and are not yet in heaven. Therefore, this also proves that even after the Lord's ascension, Paradise is still under the earth and has not been removed to heaven.

Acts 2:34 says, "David did not ascend into the heavens." Those who hold the view that Paradise has been transferred say that at the time of the resurrection and ascension of the Lord Jesus, He removed Paradise from Hades to the heavens. There is no doubt that David should be in Hades. If Paradise had been removed to the heavens, David surely also had gone to the heavens. However, even after the Lord's ascension, up to the day of Pentecost, Peter stood up and still said that David had not ascended into the heavens.

Therefore, I want to boldly tell the brothers and sisters that up to this day only one person has ascended to the heavens, and this One is Jesus of Nazareth. Perhaps some will say, "Did not Elijah and Enoch also ascend to the heavens?" However, the Lord Jesus said to Nicodemus, "No one has ascended into heaven, but He who descended out of heaven, the Son of Man, who is in heaven" (John 3:13). There had never been a man in heaven. Now in heaven there is only one man, the Lord Jesus who died and resurrected. This One is not a disembodied spirit; He is a perfect man who has been clothed with a resurrected body. The Bible tells us that David has not yet ascended to the heavens. His body is left on earth, and his soul is comforted in Paradise, the pleasant section of Hades.

Let us go on to read 2 Corinthians 5:1-3: "For we know that if our earthly tabernacle dwelling is taken down, we have a building from God, a dwelling not made with hands, eternal, in the heavens. For also in this we groan, longing to be clothed upon with our dwelling place from heaven, if indeed, being clothed, we will not be found naked." Here the earthly tabernacle refers to our physical body, whereas the eternal dwelling in the heavens refers to our resurrected body, our transfigured body, which will be raptured. Let me ask you, is Paul clothed with such a resurrected body? What about Peter? What about all the saved ones who died throughout the centuries? It is clear that they all have not been clothed with such a resurrected body. What if they were found to be unclothed? We have said earlier that disembodied spirits are abnormal. Hence, those who have died and have not been resurrected may not be brought to the heavens. Disembodied spirits, those who have the lingering scent of death, cannot be in the heavens. God has to put them in another place where they will be comforted and wait to be clothed with a resurrected body.

Therefore, Paul said, "For also in this [tabernacle] we groan, longing to be clothed upon with our dwelling place from heaven, if indeed, being clothed, we will not be found naked. For also, we who are in this tabernacle groan, being burdened, in that we do not desire to be unclothed, but clothed upon" (vv. 2-4a). To be unclothed means to die, and to be clothed is to be transfigured. Paul's desire was not to be unclothed but to be clothed upon, that is, to have what is mortal swallowed up by life (v. 4b).

I believe the brothers and sisters are clearer now. However, there are two other verses in the Scriptures that easily stir up arguments and therefore also require our attention. One is Philippians 1:23. There Paul says that he had "the desire to depart and be with Christ, for this is far better." Based on this verse, some have said, "If this is not going to a heavenly mansion, then what is it? You say that the believers are in Hades after they die, but Paul said that when believers die they are with Christ and that it is far better. How do you explain this? Can someone be with Christ and yet not be in the heavenly mansion?"

This is our answer: A person can be with the Lord without going to a heavenly mansion. To be with the Lord is a relative matter and not an absolute one. Even today, we are with the Lord. Therefore, this is a matter of degree. We may not use the fact that a person is with the Lord to conclude that he is in a heavenly mansion. To make a conclusion on this matter we need to refer to the words of the entire Bible.

We all know that our body is physical and our spirit is spiritual. When our spirit is still in our body, we are in the physical world. At this time, even though we have the Lord's presence in our spirit, this presence is very limited due to the restriction of the physical world. However, after we die and are freed from the physical world, on the one hand, we become disembodied spirits, but on the other hand, we are also freed from the restriction of the physical world and enter into the spiritual world. At such a time, our being with the Lord, of course, will be much closer than in the physical world.

Therefore, to be with the Lord does not prove that we will be in a heavenly mansion with the Lord. What it means is that we will depart from the physical world and enter into a spiritual world to have more enjoyment of being with the Lord. Let me use a little illustration. Today we all are in China, but perhaps next month you will go to America. America has numerous cities, such as New York and San Francisco. Although you are in America, you may not be in New York but in San Francisco. Generally speaking, you are in America; specifically speaking, you are in one of the numerous places in America. Likewise, when we depart from the physical world and enter into the spiritual world, it does not necessarily mean that we are in one particular place.

Another verse in the Scriptures is 1 Thessalonians 4:14, which says, "For if we believe that Jesus died and rose, so also those who have fallen asleep through Jesus, God will bring with Him." Some may respond, "You say that the saved ones who died did not go to heaven, but here it says clearly that the Lord Jesus will bring them with Him at His coming back. When the Lord Jesus comes back, does He not come back from heaven? Therefore, according to this verse, today they are already with the Lord in heaven."

To resolve this problem, I would ask you to read the text following this verse: "For this we say to you by the word of the Lord, that we who are living, who are left remaining unto the coming of the Lord, shall by no means precede those who have fallen asleep; because the Lord Himself, with a shout of command, with the voice of the archangel and with the trumpet of God, will descend from heaven" (vv. 15-16a). Indeed, when the Lord comes back, He comes back from heaven. Verse 16 concludes, "And the dead in Christ will rise first." Here the Greek text says "will rise," not "will resurrect." Please take note that verse 14 says that they will be brought with the Lord Jesus, while this verse says that they will "rise" first. Verse 17 says, "Then we who are living, who are left remaining, will be caught up together with them in the clouds to meet the Lord in the air; and thus we will be always with the Lord."

I believe that by reading these verses, you brothers and sisters are clear that when the Lord comes back, first those who have fallen asleep in the Lord (those who are dead) will rise, and then they will be caught up together with the living believers. If the dead believers are already in heaven waiting for the Lord to bring them with Him at His coming back, do they still need to rise? That would not be a rising but a descending.

The actual meaning of this portion of the Word is that, up to the time of the Lord's coming, the bodies of all the dead saints are still in the earth, and their spirits are in Paradise, in the heart of the earth. Therefore, when the Lord Jesus descends from heaven in His coming back, their bodies will rise from the earth, and their spirits will also come out from Paradise in Hades to be clothed with a resurrected body. Then they, together with the transfigured living ones, will be caught up to the clouds to meet the Lord. You see, here it still says that they are to meet the Lord. This also proves that they have not met the Lord before His coming.

Here it says that God will bring them with Jesus. This is not hard to understand either. When the Lord Jesus comes again, that is also the time of the resurrection of the dead believers, so they will come with the Lord Jesus. Whatever time the Lord Jesus comes back, that will also be the time of their coming back. At the time of the coming of the Lord Jesus, just as God will bring the Lord Jesus, so also He will bring the dead believers with the Lord. These things provide even less proof that the dead believers are with the Lord Jesus in heaven. Suppose your father is in America and your mother is in Japan. On the day that your father comes back, your mother will also come back with him. Can the fact of their coming back together prove that your mother was in the same place as your father? The answer is obvious.

Furthermore, here it says clearly that the Lord Jesus and the dead believers are in two places. On the one hand, it says the Lord Jesus will descend from heaven, and on the other hand, it says He will come with the dead believers. He will not descend at once to the earth. He will first descend to the air, and then the dead believers will rise out of the earth to be resurrected and transfigured, and they will be caught up together with the living believers to the clouds to meet the Lord. Hence, here you see the comings from two directions. The Lord Jesus will come down from the heavens, and the dead believers will rise and come out of the earth.

I believe that by now the brothers and sisters should be clear that today the believers who died are still in Paradise in the heart of the earth waiting for the Lord's coming. At the time of the Lord's coming, they will rise out of the heart of the earth and be clothed with a resurrected body to become one complete person. On that day, before God they will be altogether free from death, clothed with a glorious body, and caught up to the heavens to be with the Lord forever. However, do not forget that the rapture to the air at that time is but for a moment, because the New Jerusalem will still descend from heaven (Rev. 21:2). Therefore, our eternal habitation is not in heaven.

A CONCLUDING WORD

We have to see that the dwelling place God has prepared for us in His salvation is not in heaven. The dwelling place God has prepared for us is God Himself. God's desire is to save us into Himself that we may take Him as our habitation. Unlike today's degraded and deformed Christianity, God does not give much attention to a heavenly mansion. In the original text of the Bible there is "heaven" but no "heavenly mansion." In the Chinese version of the Bible, "heavenly mansion" is mentioned twice, once in Hebrews 9:24 and again in 1 Peter 3:22. In both places the original text is "heaven." Heaven is mentioned many, many times in the Scriptures, but I do not know why the translators of the Chinese version rendered it "heavenly mansion" in these two places in particular. "Heavenly mansion" is a term used in Buddhism. In the holy Scriptures there is only heaven, which is the third heaven, the present dwelling place of God. One day all the dead believers will be resurrected, and the living ones will be transfigured, and they all will be clothed with a glorious body and be with the Lord. Afterwards, the New Jerusalem will descend from heaven, and God will dwell with us in the New Jerusalem for eternity. Hence, it is the New Jerusalem that will be the eternal habitation of God and us.

This is a mysterious matter which we cannot comprehend thoroughly. Our dwelling place is God Himself, and God's dwelling place is we the saved ones. If you read Revelation 21, you can see a city there, but you cannot see the people who dwell in it, because the dwellers are the city itself. Peter is one of the foundations, and so is John. The twelve apostles are the twelve foundations. Therefore, you can see that those who dwell in the city are the city itself. God is our habitation, and we are also His habitation.

May God have mercy on us that we may see that the desire of God is to save us into Himself that we may take Him as our dwelling place. At the same time, God also desires to dwell in us and take us as His eternal habitation. Therefore, whether we are on this earth or in Paradise, it is temporary. Just as the earth is a place of our sojourning, so also Paradise in Hades is a place where we receive temporary comfort. Even the day we are clothed with a glorious body and are caught up to the air will be but a moment. Our eternal dwelling place is the New Jerusalem, which is produced by the mingling of God and man.

CHAPTER SEVEN

MATURITY AND BUILDING

(1)

Matthew 3:12 says, "Whose winnowing fan is in His hand. And He will thoroughly cleanse His threshing floor and will gather His wheat into His barn, but the chaff He will burn up with unquenchable fire." The Lord Himself, the Lord of the harvest, is the One who cleanses the threshing floor. He will thoroughly cleanse His threshing floor and will gather His wheat into His barn. The wheat signifies those who truly belong to the Lord. The Lord likens those who belong to Him to the harvest.

Verse 3 of chapter thirteen says, "And He spoke many things to them in parables, saying, Behold, the sower went out to sow." Verses 8 and 9 say, "But others fell on the good earth and yielded fruit, one a hundredfold, and one sixtyfold, and one thirtyfold. He who has ears to hear, let him hear." In this parable of sowing, the Lord shows us more clearly that those whom He saved are His harvest He produced with the seed of life.

Verses 24-26 say, "Another parable He set before them, saying, The kingdom of the heavens has become like a man sowing good seed in his field. But while the men slept, his enemy came and sowed tares in the midst of the wheat and went away. And when the blade sprouted and produced fruit, then the tares appeared also." Verse 30 says, "Let both grow together until the harvest, and at the time of the harvest I will say to the reapers, Collect first the tares and bind them into bundles to burn them up, but the wheat gather into my barn." Chapter three refers to the matter of gathering the wheat into the barn. Chapter thirteen again mentions gathering the wheat into the barn.

Verses 37 and 38 say, "And He answered and said, He who sows the good seed is the Son of Man; and the field is the world; and the good seed, these are the sons of the kingdom; and the tares are the sons of the evil one." Please note that the field here is the world, not the church. The tares and the wheat grow together in the world, not in the church. Regrettably, however, many people in Christianity interpret the field as the church, saying that the tares and the wheat grow together in the church. Yet the Lord clearly says that the field is the world and the tares grow in the world. The wheat signifies the genuine saved ones, who also live in the world. Here the wheat is the church. The church is not a place; the world is a place. The church is the wheat; it is something living.

Verses 39-43 say, "And the enemy who sowed them is the devil; and the harvest is the consummation of the age; and the reapers are angels. Therefore just as the tares are collected and burned up with fire, so will it be at the consummation of the age. The Son of Man will send His angels, and they will collect out of His kingdom all the stumbling blocks and those who practice lawlessness, and will cast them into the furnace of fire. In that place there will be the weeping and the gnashing of teeth. Then the righteous will shine forth like the sun in the kingdom of their Father."

If you read the context, you will be clear that the righteous are the wheat gathered into the barn. This is also the Lord's explanation of the parable. The Lord first spoke the parable to the crowd and then explained it to the disciples. After He told them what the field is, who sows the good seed, and who sows the tares, He told them what the outcome of the wheat and the tares will be. The wheat signifies the righteous; their outcome is that they will shine forth like the sun in the kingdom of their Father. These words tell us that in the eyes of God, His people in this age are like the harvest growing in the field.

First Corinthians 3:5-9 says, "What then is Apollos? And what is Paul? Ministers through whom you believed, even as the Lord gave to each one of them. I planted, Apollos watered, but God caused the growth. So then neither is he who plants anything nor he who waters, but God who causes the growth. Now he who plants and he who waters are one, but each will receive his own reward according to his own labor. For we are God's fellow workers; you are God's cultivated land, God's building." *Cultivated land* can also be translated as "farm." In this portion the apostle puts *farm* and *building* together. On the one hand, the believers are God's farm, God's cultivated land; on the other hand, they are God's house, God's building. On the one hand, the work of the apostles is planting and watering, which naturally refers to the aspect of the farm. On the other hand, the saints are God's house, God's building, so the apostle says that their work is also a building work.

Verses 10 through 13 say, "According to the grace of God given to me, as a wise master builder I have laid a foundation, and another builds upon it. But let each man take heed how he builds upon it. For another foundation no one is able to lay besides that which is laid, which is Jesus Christ. But if anyone builds upon the foundation gold, silver, precious stones, wood, grass, stubble, the work of each will become manifest; for the day will declare it, because it is revealed by fire, and the fire itself will prove each one's work, of what sort it is." Gold, silver, and precious stones are of one category; wood, grass, and stubble are of another. The *day* in verse 13 is the day of the Lord's coming. Verses 14 to 17 continue, "If anyone's work which he has built upon the foundation remains, he will receive a reward; if anyone's work is consumed, he will suffer loss, but he himself will be saved, yet so as through fire. Do you not know that you are the temple of God, and that the Spirit of God dwells in you? If anyone destroys the temple of God, God will destroy him; for the temple of God is holy, and such are you." Only the work of gold, silver, and precious stones can remain through fire. The work that is consumed is the work of wood, grass, and stubble. Verse 15 speaks of suffering loss and of being saved; these are two different things.

If you read from the preceding section, you will realize that *temple* in verses 16 and 17 refers to the building in verses 10-14, not to our body being the temple of God. Our body being the temple of God is not mentioned until chapter six. In chapter one and chapter three, the apostle spoke about divisions among the Corinthians. Their divisions were destroying the temple of God, so the apostle warned them here, saying that if anyone destroys the temple of God, God will destroy him.

I would like the brothers and sisters to see that in the eyes of God His people in this age are His farm, on the one hand, and His building, on the other. In order for us to know God's building, we need to pay attention to these two aspects. In regard to a farm, it needs to grow; in regard to a building, it needs to be built. Actually, the two are one, because spiritual growth is building. We know that God's spiritual building is not a dead building but a living building. Peter said, "You yourselves also, as living stones, are being built up as a spiritual house" (1 Pet. 2:5). Since these stones are living, if they do not grow, they cannot be built. To be built together, these stones have to grow. Therefore, the building is the growth, and the growth is the building.

Revelation 14:1 says, "And I saw, and behold, the Lamb standing on Mount Zion, and with Him a hundred and forty-four thousand, having His name and the name of His Father written on their foreheads." Verses 4 and 5 say, "These are they who follow the Lamb wherever He may go. These were purchased from among men as firstfruits to God and to the Lamb. And in their mouth no lie was found; they are without blemish." These verses show us a group of people who are firstfruits to God. We know this word is quoted from Leviticus 23 in the Old Testament. The firstfruits are a small part of the harvest which ripens first.

Verses 14-16 say, "And I saw, and behold, there was a white cloud, and on the cloud One like the Son of Man sitting, having a golden crown on His head and a sharp sickle in His hand. And another angel came out of the temple, crying with a loud voice to Him who sat on the cloud, Send forth Your sickle and reap, for the hour to reap has come because the harvest of the earth is ripe. And He who sat on the cloud thrust His sickle upon the earth, and the earth was reaped." Please pay attention to the end of verse 15—the prerequisite for the reaping is being ripe. The preceding verses speak about firstfruits; verses 14 through 16 speak about the harvest. The firstfruits are a fraction, whereas the harvest is the whole. Whether it is the firstfruits or the harvest, the principle and requirement are that it should be fully ripe. The first to ripen are gathered first; these are the firstfruits. When all are fully ripened, that will be the time of reaping.

THE ETERNAL DWELLING PLACE OF GOD AND MAN BEING THE BUILDING OF THE MINGLING OF GOD WITH MAN

I believe that after reading these messages everyone is able to clearly see that for us the saved ones, our eternal dwelling place is not in any of the three places of the universe—heaven, earth, or underneath the earth. We often say that the earth is where we dwell as pilgrims. Even people in the world confess that human life is a pilgrimage. The earth is where man passes through in his journey as a pilgrim. Underneath the earth is Hades, and within it is Paradise, the place of Abraham's bosom where the souls of the deceased saints are comforted. That also is not the eternal dwelling place of the saved ones. When the Lord comes again, the souls of the dead saints will rise from Paradise in Hades, put on a resurrected and transfigured body, and then be caught up together in the air with the living and remaining saints to meet the Lord. Later, the holy city New Jerusalem will descend from heaven, and then God will dwell with us forever. So even heaven is not the eternal dwelling place of the saints. Our eternal dwelling place is the New Jerusalem, and the New Jerusalem will descend from heaven at the time of the new heaven and new earth.

Many of the hymns in Christianity mention heaven being our home. This is an erroneous concept. From the time of our resurrection and rapture to the descending of the New Jerusalem from heaven, there will be at most one thousand years. The human concept is that God's intention is to save and bring man to a certain place. In reading God's Word, however, you can realize that God does not have a place as the goal, but the goal is He Himself. God's intention is to save man into Himself. God has this as the goal of His salvation.

This is not merely a matter of God's salvation, but also a

matter of God's eternal purpose. The eternal purpose of God is that man be mingled with Him. This is why we always say that God is working Himself into man and working man into Himself. It is not a matter of time or space but a matter of person. Therefore, the Bible shows us repeatedly that God wants to be mingled with man and take man as His dwelling place. God says, "Heaven is My throne, / And the earth the footstool for My feet. / ...Where is the place of My rest?" (Isa. 66:1). What His heart cares for and what He wants to gain are those of a contrite spirit, who tremble at His word (v. 2). Therefore, neither heaven nor earth is the place of His rest; it is man who is His resting place. Nevertheless, those who knew God in the Old Testament times revealed their longings through their groaning and prayer. They desired to dwell in the house of God all the days of their lives (Psa. 23:6; 27:4). They realized that there was not a place in the universe where they could dwell. God alone was their dwelling place.

All of the foregoing verses reveal that God's desire is to have man as His habitation and to have man take Him as his habitation. That is why in the New Testament you see many *in*s, especially in the Gospel of John: "In that day you will know that I am in My Father, and you in Me, and I in you" (14:20). This is God dwelling in man that man may also dwell in God. Therefore, when we come to 1 John, we read such a word: "In this we know that we abide in Him and He in us, that He has given to us of His Holy Spirit" (4:13). His giving to us of the Holy Spirit is His pouring of oil upon us as stones (Gen. 28:18-19a). This is Bethel, the house of God. Through the Holy Spirit's entering into us, God abides in us and we in Him. This is the house of God.

THE HOUSE IN WHICH BOTH GOD AND MAN DWELL BEING NOT A PLACE BUT A PERSON

The first step in this matter was the Lord's incarnation. This was the first step of God's entering into man. John says very clearly that the Lord's becoming flesh was His tabernacling among men. Later, the Lord Himself also said that the body of His incarnation was the temple of God, or we may say, the house of God. The Jews wanted to destroy the Lord's body, but the Lord said, "Destroy this temple, and in three days I will raise it up" (2:19). This means that the Lord would raise this temple up in resurrection. We have said that the body crucified by the Jews was limited to only one man, Jesus the Nazarene, but the Body raised up by the Lord through resurrection includes millions of His believers. When a grain of wheat dies, it bears much fruit (12:24). Before the grain dies, it is just a single grain; after its death and resurrection, it grows into many grains. Therefore, the Lord's word in John 2, "Destroy this temple, and in three days I will raise it up," is a great word. We cannot understand it merely according to letter; we need spiritual understanding. God obtained a house on earth by putting on humanity and dwelling in humanity. This is the house that Satan attempted to destroy through man. However, the Lord said that He would raise it up in resurrection. This word will be fully fulfilled when we are raptured in the future. Then we will see that this temple, this house, this Body, which the Lord raised up in resurrection, is not just one individual—Jesus the Nazarene—but includes all who were regenerated through His death and resurrection throughout the ages.

Therefore, this house of God is not a place but a corporate person. This house is composed of the Triune God and all the saved ones. The apostolic Epistles express the same thought. Peter said, "You...as living stones, are being built up as a spiritual house" (1 Pet. 2:5). Paul said, "In whom you also are being built together into a dwelling place of God in spirit" (Eph. 2:22). These verses show us that this building is not a place but an entity composed of God and man.

I believe the brothers and sisters are already quite clear concerning this point. Now we will make still another turn. If we look at it simply from Hebrews 11, it seems that the city Abraham, Isaac, and Jacob longed after is a place. However, when we come to Hebrews 12, we realize that the name of the city is the heavenly Jerusalem. Therefore, what they eagerly waited for is the holy city of God, the heavenly Jerusalem. However, when you read on to Revelation, you see that the holy city is not a place. This is because the city is the bride, the wife of the Lamb. On the one hand, she is God's tabernacle, that which is built by God to be the eternal dwelling place of God and man. On the other hand, she is also the bride of the Lamb, the counterpart whom Christ has gained. Therefore, you must agree that this is not a matter of place but a matter of person. This city is the group of people God has built throughout the generations, composed of the Old Testament saints represented by the twelve tribes and the New Testament saints represented by the twelve apostles.

Now we turn back to look at John 14. The Lord said, "In My Father's house are many abodes" (v. 2). Now we know that this is not what people generally refer to as the heavenly mansion. Many people say that the Father's house in John 14 is the holy city in Hebrews 11. This we absolutely agree with. Yet we have to ask, is the holy city in Hebrews 11 a heavenly mansion, or is it something built with God's redeemed people? The Bible does not say that this is a heavenly mansion, but Revelation 21 clearly shows us that this holy city is a city built with God's redeemed ones. This city is the Father's house. So "My Father's house" in John 14 does not denote heaven or a heavenly mansion. Rather, it denotes a building, which is God taking man as His dwelling place and bringing man into God that man may take God as his dwelling place.

Therefore, from John 14:2 through chapter seventeen, all that the Lord spoke about was that He would go through death and resurrection to bring man, who was outside of God, into God. The Lord said, "Where I am you also may be" (14:3). The Lord was in the Father, and through His death and resurrection we were brought into the Father as He was in the Father. That is why the Lord said that in that day "because I live, you also shall live" (v. 19). "In that day you will know that I am in My Father, and you in Me, and I in you" (v. 20). "The one who loves Me...I...will manifest Myself to him...and We will come to him and make an abode with him" (vv. 21-23). *Abode* here is the same Greek word translated as *abodes* in verse 2. So the abodes in verse 2 clearly refer not to a physical place but to those whom God gained to be His dwelling place.

Now we have made this great turn. As a result of this turn, we see that the New Jerusalem is not heaven but the people God has saved throughout the ages as His dwelling place and

His counterpart. God is not marrying a place as His counterpart; He is marrying His redeemed as His counterpart. In 2 Corinthians 11 Paul said, "I betrothed you to one husband to present you as a pure virgin to Christ" (v. 2). The counterpart of God and Christ is not a place but a group of people. This group of people becomes the dwelling place of God.

Brothers and sisters, interpreting the Bible is not a simple matter. It requires the entire Bible to interpret one verse. You cannot make a decision merely by examining one portion of the Word. If you read only Hebrews 11, it may seem to you that the city Abraham, Isaac, and Jacob eagerly waited for is a place; but if you study the entire Bible, you will see that the city is not a place but a group of people.

THE BUILDING OF GOD BEING ACCOMPLISHED BY GOD AS MAN'S LIFE GROWING AND MATURING IN MAN

If we have the light, we can see right away that God's salvation is not to save us from earth to heaven but to save us who are outside of God into God. This is the work God has been doing throughout the ages since creation. In the Bible this work is called building. God wants to build Himself into man and build man into Himself.

We know that this building work of God is accomplished by His coming to be man's life. This building of God is the pouring of oil upon the stones, as we mentioned before. The stones are we the saved ones, and the oil is the Spirit of God, the transfiguration of God, God Himself. In eternity God was the Father. When He was manifested among men, He was the Son. When He enters into man to be mingled with man and to be man's life, He is the Spirit. Therefore, the Holy Spirit is the One in whom God has a relationship with man. Oil being poured upon stones makes us living stones to be built into a living building.

The Bible uses another way to depict God's entering into us to be our life. It says that the life of God is the seed of life. First John 3:9 says plainly that God's seed abides in us. A seed contains life. God being life in us is just like a seed. Therefore, the Lord Jesus said that He was a grain of wheat.

If He did not fall into the ground and die, He would abide alone; but if He died, He would bear much fruit (John 12:24). Through His resurrection the Lord regenerated us, making us alive from within. Since then, we are God's wheat, God's crop, growing in the field of the world.

Please remember that this growth is the building. In regard to a farm, it is a matter of growth; in regard to a building, it is a matter of building. The two matters are one. If you do not grow, you cannot be built. If you grow a little, then you can be built up a little more in the church. If you grow into Christ, the Head, in a certain matter, then in that matter you can be built up with the saints. When all of us have grown and matured, this building of God will be accomplished.

I would ask you, brothers and sisters, are you God's farm, God's harvest? I believe you would all acknowledge that you are. However, I would further ask, are you mature? If you have not matured, and if the Lord comes today, do you think He will reap you? Only when the harvest is fully ripened will it be reaped and gathered into the barn. What will you do since you have not ripened? Today Christianity tells people that they will go to heaven if they believe in Jesus. I do not know what kind of thought or concept this is. They say that this is due to the efficacy of the Lord's blood. Please remember that redemption through the blood is only one aspect of God's salvation. There is another aspect, which is the aspect of life. It is true that the blood solved all of our problems before God and brought us to God. However, please remember that it is the growth in life that causes us to grow into God. God does not consider us as glass vessels that are good enough if He merely washes us clean with the blood and places us before Him. He has washed us with the blood, but He also wants to come into us to be our life that we may become a living harvest. This living harvest needs to grow and mature.

Let me ask you: Is there a lord of the harvest who reaps the crops that are still green in the field? No, the crops must be ripe before they can be gathered into the house. Now we understand that the house is the New Jerusalem. The house is the destination of the harvest after it is fully ripened. This does not refer to a heavenly mansion; it refers to the New

Jerusalem. The New Jerusalem is the ultimate destination of us who are saved. However, those who are immature cannot yet go into the house.

Therefore, we should not believe the erroneous doctrines in Christianity. They say that after a person believes in Jesus, he is washed in the blood and will go to heaven after death. This is an inaccurate statement. It is true that if you believe in the Lord Jesus, His blood washes away your sins, and when you die your spirit and soul can be comforted in Paradise in Hades. Yet I still have to ask, have you grown and matured since you were saved? Paul could say that he was matured. In 1 Corinthians 9 Paul said, "I therefore run in this way, not as though without a clear aim; I box in this way, not as though beating the air...lest perhaps having preached to others [which is preaching to others concerning maturity, concerning the gaining of the reward], I myself may become disapproved" (vv. 26-27). When he wrote Philippians, he was already quite old. At that time he was locked away in a Roman prison, and he still said, "I do not account of myself to have laid hold...Forgetting the things which are behind and stretching forward to the things which are before, I pursue toward the goal" (3:13-14). That pursuit is the growth, and it is the building. As crops, we need to grow. As a building, we need to be built. We are all running a race on a course, so we need to pursue. Even in his old age Paul said that he was pursuing.

However, in 2 Timothy 4 he said that he was about to be martyred for the Lord: "For I am already being poured out, and the time of my departure is at hand. I have fought the good fight; I have finished the course; I have kept the faith. Henceforth there is laid up for me the crown of righteousness" (vv. 6-8). He knew that he had matured. I ask you brothers and sisters, if today you were to depart from the world and your spirit went to be in Abraham's bosom, would you be able to say what Paul said? Paul could say that he had matured and was waiting for the Lord's coming. Can you say the same thing? Therefore, with regard to being washed by the precious blood, you are a redeemed person; you can come before God. However, you need to keep in mind that there is another aspect; that is, God's life needs to grow within you. God needs to build you into His building. Have you matured? Have you been built? This is a great matter.

CHAPTER EIGHT

MATURITY AND BUILDING

(2)

Ephesians 4:11-13 says, "And He Himself gave some as apostles and some as prophets and some as evangelists and some as shepherds and teachers, for the perfecting of the saints unto the work of the ministry, unto the building up of the Body of Christ, until we all arrive at the oneness of the faith and of the full knowledge of the Son of God, at a full-grown man, at the measure of the stature of the fullness of Christ."

John 17:20-24 says, "And I do not ask concerning these only, but concerning those also who believe into Me through their word, that they all may be one; even as You, Father, are in Me and I in You, that they also may be in Us; that the world may believe that You have sent Me. And the glory which You have given Me I have given to them, that they may be one, even as We are one; I in them, and You in Me, that they may be perfected into one, that the world may know that You have sent Me and have loved them even as You have loved Me. Father, concerning that which You have given Me, I desire that they also may be with Me where I am, that they may behold My glory, which You have given Me, for You loved Me before the foundation of the world."

Hebrews 11:16 says, "But as it is, they long after a better country, that is, a heavenly one. Therefore God is not ashamed of them, to be called their God, for He has prepared a city for them." Revelation 21:2 says, "And I saw the holy city, New Jerusalem, coming down out of heaven from God, prepared as a bride adorned for her husband." Hebrews 11 says that God has prepared a city for them; again this verse says that the city is prepared. Verse 9 says, "I will show you the bride, the wife of the Lamb."

Verse 7 of chapter 2 says, "To him who overcomes, to him I will give to eat of the tree of life, which is in the Paradise of God." Verse 12 of chapter 3 says, "He who overcomes, him I will make a pillar in the temple of My God, and he shall by no means go out anymore, and I will write upon him the name of My God and the name of the city of My God, the New Jerusalem, which descends out of heaven from My God, and My new name."

BELIEVERS NEEDING TO MATURE
BEFORE THEY CAN BE REAPED BY GOD

We have pointed out to the brothers and sisters that on the one hand, we are God's crop and, on the other hand, we are God's building. As God's crop, we need to grow and mature; as God's building, we need to be built. Our growth as God's crop is our being built as God's building. When we have grown to maturity, we are prepared to be built. Therefore, in order to be built, we have to pay attention to growth and maturity.

If you read the Bible carefully, whether the Old Testament or the New Testament, whenever the harvest is mentioned, a great emphasis is put on the matter of maturity, because only the ripened harvest can be gathered into the barn. Yet there is a sequence to the ripening of the harvest, so the Bible mentions the firstfruits and the reaping of the majority. Revelation 14 clearly shows us that the reaping of the firstfruits to God and the reaping of the majority of the harvest are at different times. The first-ripe ones are reaped first, and then the majority of the harvest is reaped afterwards.

In Leviticus 23 there is a feast called the Feast of Firstfruits, which required people to reap a small amount of the harvest that had ripened first and bring it before God. After some time, when the majority of the harvest had ripened, it would then be reaped.

We all know that the persons, things, and events in the Old Testament are not merely the persons, things, or events themselves. Every person, thing, or event is a spiritual type.

Accordingly, Leviticus 23, in speaking about the feasts to be kept by the children of God, greatly emphasizes the firstfruits and reaping. In principle, this shows us that God's harvest must be ripened; only when it is ripe can it be reaped. Although the reaping times are different, in principle, all must be mature. The ones to ripen first are reaped first; the ones to ripen later are reaped later. The unripe ones must wait in the field until they are ripened. The harvest must be ripe before it is reaped. This is very clear in the Bible.

The account of reaping in the Old Testament points out that if we are to participate in the building of the New Jerusalem, we need to mature. We should not think that a believer, whether he has matured in life or not, will be reaped by the Lord as soon as he dies. Nor should we think that a believer has matured when he dies and therefore has been reaped by the Lord. It is ludicrous to say that once a believer dies, he has matured and has been reaped. Obviously there are many believers who have had no progress after being saved for many years; whenever you meet such ones, you sense that they are immature, tender, and often even withered. Some have died in this kind of condition. Can you believe that they have been reaped because they have matured? There is no such thing.

We have to know that death is not the solution to everything. This is as true for the believers as it is for the unbelievers. In regards to the unbelieving descendants of Adam, when they die, their bodies are left in the dust, and their souls go to Hades to be tormented while they are waiting for the coming of the great day of judgment. Therefore, their death today is merely the end of one stage. The day they will be cast into the lake of fire will be the conclusion. In the same principle, the death of the believers today is not the conclusion. It is true that when a believer dies, his body is left in the earth, and his soul is comforted in Paradise in Hades. However, his problems are not yet solved; he has to wait until the coming resurrection. When the Lord comes again, all the saved ones will resurrect and stand before the judgment seat of Christ to be judged. This judgment is not the judgment of the great white throne, which determines whether you are saved or will perish. This judgment at the judgment seat of Christ is to determine whether you have matured or not, whether you will receive a reward or suffer loss. If you receive a reward, it is because you have matured. If you suffer loss, it is because you have not matured.

What if you have not matured? Please remember that God has a way to make you mature. After all, if you are not ripened, God cannot gather you into the barn. Therefore, by no means should you assume that believers can live meaninglessly and carelessly their whole life, and yet when they die, the precious blood of Christ will bear all their responsibilities. There is not such a thing. It is true that no one can come before God without being redeemed by the precious blood. The blood reconciles us to God so that we may approach God. However, please remember that those who can be reaped into the eternal house of God, those who can eternally abide in the house of God, are those who have allowed God's life to grow and mature within them. To be redeemed by the blood is one thing; to grow and mature in life is another. Only those who are fully ripened can be gathered into God's barn in the future. You should by no means think that since you are saved, you are already a living stone and therefore have already become part of the building. A stone cannot be built in unless it has been dealt with.

As I have said elsewhere, a local church is a built-up entity, but it is often in a condition of not having been fully built. For instance, a church may have two hundred brothers and sisters, yet it rests altogether on the shoulders of only fifty of them. It seems that only the fifty have been built, while the remaining one hundred fifty are like materials that are piled next to a building and are not yet built up. However, in eternity, in the new heaven and new earth, you will not find a pile of materials around the city of New Jerusalem. All who are represented by the twelve tribes and by the twelve apostles will have been built into the city.

I will not discuss, for the time being, at what point in time all these people are built into the city. However, I have to say that you surely are not built into it as soon as you die after living a meaningless life as a carefree Christian. There is no such thing. I say again that as the harvest, you need to be ripened, and as the building, you need to be built. You are a sheaf on God's farm. You need to grow and mature, and only then can God reap you into His barn. You are also one of the stones to be used by God. You need to be dealt with and built up in order to be fitted into the building of God.

In His last evening with the disciples, after the Lord Jesus spoke to them about the union between Him and them, He prayed for all those who believed in Him. What did He pray? He prayed to the Father that they all may be one. Please remember that in this prayer the Lord asked God to bring all whom He redeemed throughout the ages into God one by one to build them into one entity, to become one. Strictly speaking, this oneness is the building of God. This oneness does not come out of our calling to each other, "Come! Let us be one." This will not work. Oneness comes out of God's building. Consider a physical house; the many materials in it are one. Formerly all these materials were scattered about in piles and were not one at all. It is by being built that they have become one. Therefore, the building is the oneness. All those who are in the Lord will one day be one in the Triune God. This was the intent of the Lord's prayer.

Now I would like to ask you, are you one with all the others who are saved? There is no need to speak of being one with all who are saved; sometimes even five people—two responsible brothers and three responsible sisters of a home meeting—cannot have oneness among themselves. Why is this? It is because they have not been built. Now please consider, as such a one who has not been built and who cannot be one with God's children, when you leave this world one day, can you then immediately be in the New Jerusalem? You certainly cannot.

Therefore, will the prayer of the Lord not be fulfilled? We should believe that eventually the Lord's prayer will not be in vain and will be fulfilled in the universe. Eventually, we will see that all who belong to the Lord will be absolutely one in Him. Paul believed this. He said that the Lord has given various gifts for the building up of the Body of Christ, until we all arrive at the oneness of the faith and of the full knowledge of the Son of God, at a full-grown man, at the measure of the stature of the fullness of Christ (Eph. 4:11-13). You can see how great the apostle's faith was when he spoke this word! When he wrote the Epistle to the Ephesians, he was locked away in a Roman prison. He also saw how very desolate the churches were in all the places. Not only were they desolate; they even rejected his teaching. All who were in Asia would turn away from him. This was becoming the situation when he wrote Ephesians. Yet he could still say, "Until we all arrive at the oneness of the faith and of the full knowledge of the Son of God, at a full-grown man, at the measure of the stature of the fullness of Christ." Consider how strong Paul's faith was! What he believed was completely contrary to what he saw, but he could still joyfully declare this.

Therefore, we do not have to be worried. One day the Lord's prayer will be fulfilled. With men this is impossible, but with God all things are possible (Matt. 19:26). God always has a way. Nevertheless, since you are a saved one, you have to grow, mature, and be built. If you do not mature in this age, God still has the next age waiting for you. In any case, He will cause you to mature. If you, being the harvest, are not ripened today, tomorrow God will cause the sun to scorch you. If you are not ripened, God will have to leave you in the field. If you are not ripe, you cannot be gathered into the barn. Do not be deceived by the erroneous doctrine in Christianity, thinking that you will go to heaven immediately after your death if you believe in Jesus. If you want to be in God's barn, you need to be matured. Please read your New Testament again so you may be clear that this is a fixed principle. It is true that everyone who has been washed by the Lord's blood will eternally be saved and will not perish forever. However, in order to go to God, enter into God's dwelling place, and be gathered into God's barn, one must be matured. Sooner or later, one will nevertheless be matured. This is a fixed principle.

THE PROCESS OF THE BUILDING OF GOD
IN THE WRITINGS OF JOHN

We have pointed out repeatedly that the issue of God's work throughout the ages is to gain a city, the New Jerusalem. This is stated clearly in the writings of John. John wrote his Gospel, he also wrote his Epistles, and in the end he wrote the book of Revelation. The messages conveyed in these three sections are connected and cannot be separated. Therefore, if you want to understand the writings of John, you cannot just read his Gospel, nor can you read only his Epistles, and in the same way you cannot read only his Revelation. You have to read these three parts of his writings together to see a complete picture.

In the beginning John says that God became flesh and tabernacled among men (John 1:14). Later, he says that this tabernacle built through incarnation was a temple, the house of God (2:21). Satan wanted to destroy this temple, but the Lord raised it up through resurrection (v. 19). After that he also says that he who has the bride is the bridegroom (3:29). The Lord, who was incarnated, who tabernacled among men, who built up the temple, is the Bridegroom.

Now you can see that there is the tabernacle, there is the temple (which is the house), and there is the Bridegroom, who comes for the bride. What is this tabernacle? What is this house? Who is this bride? It is hard to understand in the beginning. However, if you read on, you will come to the verse in which the Lord says, "Abide in Me and I in you" (15:4). This word has a twofold meaning. On the one hand, it concerns our mutual abiding with the Lord; this is a matter of the house. On the other hand, it concerns our mutual union with the Lord; that is a matter of the bride and Bridegroom. Please keep in mind that John 14, 15, 16, and 17 talk about these matters. After the Lord resurrected from the dead and breathed into the disciples, when the Holy Spirit entered into them, the Lord Himself entered into them. Then the Lord in reality had an abode in the disciples. From that time on, the house came into existence.

In John's first Epistle, he says, we "report to you the eternal life...that you also may have fellowship...with the Father and with His Son" (1:2-3). "The anointing which you have received from Him abides in you,...and even as it has taught you, abide in Him [the Lord]" (2:27). "We know that we abide in Him [God] and He in us, that He [God] has given to us of

His Spirit" (4:13). "This [eternal] life is in His Son. He who has the Son has the life; he who does not have the Son of God does not have the life" (5:11-12). "The Son of God has come and has given us an understanding that we might know Him who is true; and we are in Him who is true, in His Son Jesus Christ. This is the true God" (v. 20). This true God implies the whole story of God in His incarnation, death, resurrection, entering into man as the Spirit, and becoming man's life. In the Old Testament times, God was simply God. However, in the New Testament time this God became flesh, died and resurrected, and also entered into us as the Spirit to be joined to us. All these steps are implied in "the true God." Now we are more clear.

When we read to the end of Revelation, we see a city coming forth. This city is the tabernacle God has built among men. This city is also the bride of the Lamb. Now we have found everything that John speaks of from the beginning to the end. He says that he who has the bride is the bridegroom. Who is the bride? The bride is the city. The city is also the tabernacle. At the same time, this city is the temple, because he says, "I saw no temple in it" (Rev. 21:22). The city is the enlargement of the temple. Furthermore, Revelation shows us the Triune God dwelling fully in the redeemed people. In this way, at the end of Revelation you see that the things John mentioned in the beginning have been fully fulfilled. The New Jerusalem is the tabernacle built by God. It is God's dwelling place, God's house, and God's bride. This is the central subject of the writings of John.

THE LORD STILL DOING THE BUILDING WORK IN THE KINGDOM AGE

However, I would like to point out to the brothers and sisters when the last part of the Lord's building work will be carried out. We know that the manifestation of the holy city, New Jerusalem, is the ultimate issue of God's work. This issue will be manifested only at the time of the new heaven and the new earth. All who read the Bible know that the old heaven and the old earth precede the new heaven and the new earth. In the old heaven and the old earth there are many different ages. Among these ages, a great period of time is the age of law, and the next is the age of grace. After the age of grace there is the millennial age, which is the kingdom age. The age of law began with Moses. Before Moses, there was another age, the age of the patriarchs, which is also called the age of promise. Between Christ's first coming and Christ's second coming is the age of grace, which is also called the church age. Once the church age ends, the Lord will come again, and from then on it will be the millennial age. When the millennial age ends, the old heaven and the old earth will end, and the new heaven and the new earth begin. Therefore, to us there are four ages in the old heaven and the old earth. These are the age of promise, the age of law, the age of grace, and the kingdom age. When these ages are over, the new heaven and the new earth will come. Once the new heaven and the new earth come, the New Jerusalem will be manifested.

Because the building of the New Jerusalem is carried out in the old heaven and the old earth, all of the four ages mentioned above involve the building work of God. God carried out a part of His building in the age of the patriarchs, the age of the promise. Abel, Enoch, and Noah were men whom God built; so were Abraham, Isaac, and Jacob. They were all built in the age of the patriarchs. Another part of the building of God, which consisted of the twelve tribes of Israel, was built by God in the age of law. Still another part, the church, is built by God during the age of grace.

Now I would like to ask you all, can you say that God built in the age of the patriarchs, in the age of law, and in the age of grace, yet stops building in the millennial (kingdom) age? Although the millennial age will be an age of restoration, it will still be an age in which God builds. Even though the Lord will have come and all things will be restored, the building work of God will still be incomplete at that time.

Again, this is where we come into conflict with the theology in Christianity. Their typical theology tells people that when the Lord Jesus comes again, all things will be complete; all things will rest in peace. However, we realize from reading the Bible that the Lord will still do His building work at the time of His second coming.

On one occasion a person who knew the Lord well came to ask me about the matter of saved ones being disciplined at the Lord's second coming. I said that today Christians all agree that a saved person should readily love God, do God's will, and please God. If he does not love God and does not do God's will, God will chastise and discipline him. No one in Christianity would disagree with this kind of teaching concerning God's discipline. However, I would like to ask, can it be that God's chastisement and discipline of His children are limited only to the first three ages? Or will there still be discipline in the fourth age when the Lord Jesus comes back? Today the typical Christian thinks that discipline is limited only to the present life. He never thinks that there will be discipline when the Lord comes back. Yet the Bible clearly shows us that there will still be the matter of discipline when the Lord comes back.

Please read Luke 12:45-48: "But if that slave says in his heart, My master is delaying his coming, and begins to beat the male servants and the female servants and to eat and to drink and become drunk [this is one who indulges himself wantonly, not getting along with the other servants], the master of that slave will come on a day when he does not expect him and at an hour which he does not know, and will cut him asunder, and will appoint his portion with the unbelievers. And that slave who knew his master's will and did not prepare or do according to his will, will receive many lashes; but he who did not know, yet did things worthy of stripes, will receive few lashes [not zero lashes but "few" lashes]. But to every one to whom much has been given, much will be required from him; and to whom much has been committed, they will ask of him all the more." Here it clearly says that it is when the master comes back, the slave may receive many lashes. Thus, we see that the Lord's chastisement and discipline are not limited to this age. When the Lord comes back, not only will there be discipline, but the discipline may even be greater than before.

Brothers and sisters, if you open your eyes and look, you will see that many saved ones are indulging their flesh, loving the world, and not being one with God's children. Yet they are still safe and sound; God has not disciplined them. I ask you, brothers and sisters, today among God's children are there more who obey the Lord or more who disobey the Lord? Obviously there are more disobedient ones. So then today among God's children are there more who are disciplined or more who are not disciplined? To be honest, we do not see many who are disciplined. Look at all those children of God who, after being saved for many years, still indulge in the flesh, act recklessly at will, and lose their temper and quarrel whenever they feel like it. It seems that God does not bother them and does not discipline them. Therefore, we have to admit that although many Christians disobey today, few are disciplined.

You should never think that the reason God does not discipline us is because He loves us so much that He is reluctant to discipline us. If this is what you think, you are wrong. Hebrews 12 says that whom the Lord loves He disciplines. Those who are disciplined are beloved, and those who are not disciplined are pitiful. However, do not suppose that since they are not disciplined today, they also will not be disciplined in the future. There is not one child who can avoid being disciplined, but as to when the child is disciplined, it depends on the father's own will. You know that a father who keeps his temper under control knows his timing in disciplining his children. He does not spank the child when he may lose his temper; rather, he looks for the right time. Some children need a spanking right after making a mistake, while others need to wait until the next day, and still others need to wait until the end of the semester.

I would like to tell the brothers and sisters that too many children of God are disobedient, yet hardly any have been disciplined. Rather, you see the opposite situation: Quite a few who love the Lord and learn to live before the Lord have been repeatedly afflicted and smitten. I would like to ask you, do you think that God will never discipline those disobedient children? They live as they please, not growing, not being dealt with, not being built, but going through their entire life aimlessly. Do you think that ultimately they will just die and go to heaven? Do you think God will let this happen? Of course He will not. The Lord said that when He comes back some will receive many lashes.

Please keep in mind that discipline is building. All the parents who discipline their children do so for their perfecting. Likewise, discipline from God is for building. You should never assume that the Lord does the building work, the dealing work, and the disciplining work only during the time before His coming back. The Bible clearly tells us that when the Lord comes back, He will give lashes, even many lashes. Even the giving of lashes is building. If today you are not willing to be dealt with by the Lord, when the Lord comes, you will still be dealt with. If today you are not willing to be built up by the Lord, when the Lord comes He will still build you up. Before you are dealt with, this brother does not seem lovely and that sister has problems as well; you can never be one with others. However, a day will come when the Lord will deal with you to such an extent that every brother and sister is lovely in your sight.

I believe that the brothers and sisters can understand the meaning of these words. The building of God is carried out in the four ages of the old heaven and the old earth. The building work of God is in every age. Even though during the millennial kingdom the Lord will have come and all things will be restored, it will still be the old heaven and the old earth, not the new heaven and the new earth. God will still be doing the building work. It is in the new heaven and the new earth that the building work of God will have been accomplished.

THOSE WHO ARE MATURE AND ARE BUILT UP TODAY ENJOYING THE BLESSING OF THE NEW JERUSALEM IN THE MILLENNIAL KINGDOM

However, we need to strengthen one point a little. Although the New Jerusalem will be manifested only in the new heaven and the new earth, if you read Revelation carefully, you will see the New Jerusalem in chapter two and chapter three. There the blessings promised by the Lord to the overcomers in the churches are really the things in the New Jerusalem, yet the overcomers will be able to partake of them in the millennial kingdom. This means that their enjoyment of the New

Jerusalem will come a thousand years earlier than that of the majority of the believers. They are a group of first-ripe ones. They are the ones who were built up by God in the age of the patriarchs, the age of law, and the age of grace. Only these ones will be able to enjoy the New Jerusalem in the millennial age. As for those who have not been fully built up by God, those who have not matured, God will edify them and build them in the millennial kingdom so that they can be matured. When the millennial kingdom is over, they will have been dealt with and built up, and then they will be in the New Jerusalem when the new heaven and the new earth emerge.

The Bible says that when the Lord comes again, the marriage of the Lamb will come, for His wife will have made herself ready (Rev. 19:7). When the New Jerusalem is manifested, she will be the wife of the Lamb (21:9). This shows us that the entire millennial kingdom is the Lamb's wedding day. In the millennial kingdom the New Jerusalem is the bride, and in the new heaven and the new earth the New Jerusalem is the wife. Those who participate in the New Jerusalem as the bride are the overcoming saints, the matured ones who have been dealt with and built up by the Lord. The saints who need to be built up by the Lord during the millennial kingdom will not participate in the New Jerusalem as the bride. Those who have been built by the Lord during the millennial age will have to wait until the new heaven and the new earth, when the bride has become the wife, to participate in the New Jerusalem.

I say these things so that the brothers and sisters can see that the principle of the bride is that of God's children needing to be matured and built up. If you are not matured today, the Lord will still cause you to be mature in the future. If you are not built up today, the Lord will still build you up in the future. For you and me there is the difference of time; there is a difference between today and tomorrow, the present and the future. To God, however, there is no element of time. For you and me there is the matter of space; there is the matter of being built here and not being built there, but to God there is no element of space. In any case, you will be built up; you will be matured. If you are not matured, God has no way to gather you into the barn. If you are not built up, you have no place in the building of God.

I would like to declare to God's children that according to the Bible, there is no such thing as what people in Christianity mean by "going to heaven." While you are alive, the earth is where you sojourn; when you die, Paradise in Hades will be where you stay temporarily. When you are resurrected, transfigured, and caught up in the air by the Lord, that will still be a temporary condition. Our eternal dwelling is the New Jerusalem, a city that is the issue of the mutual building of God and man. Therefore, you must grow in God and mature in God. If you are not matured, you cannot be gathered into this barn. If you are not built up, you cannot participate in this building. If today you are not matured, tomorrow God still will want you to be matured. If in this age you are not built up, God will still build you up in the next age. As long as you are saved and redeemed, God will cause you to mature and will build you up, whatever it takes. I say again that the entire Bible ultimately shows us that the redeemed people are built together to become an eternal dwelling place of God and man. Therefore, one who has not matured and not been built up can never participate in that dwelling place.

Brothers and sisters, the Bible never tells us that once a person is washed by the blood he is "going to heaven." There is not such a thing. God wants to build Himself into His redeemed people and to build His redeemed people into Himself to accomplish a spiritual building. Therefore, all who participate in this building must be those who have been built up. Thank the Lord that God predestinated us and redeemed us, and He is building us. What God has been doing for six thousand years is this building work.

Finally, I would still tell the brothers and sisters that we need to be matured. Only when we are matured can we be gathered into the barn. We need to be built; only by being built can we participate in God's holy city, the New Jerusalem. May the Lord grant us grace that we would not consider these things as mere prophecies. May we be built together today!

ABOUT THE AUTHOR

Witness Lee was born in 1905 in northern China and raised in a Christian family. At age 19 he was fully captured for Christ and immediately consecrated himself to preach the gospel for the rest of his life. Early in his service, he met Watchman Nee, a renowned preacher, teacher, and writer. Witness Lee labored together with Watchman Nee under his direction. In 1934 Watchman Nee entrusted Witness Lee with the responsibility for his publication operation, called the Shanghai Gospel Bookroom.

Prior to the Communist takeover in 1949, Witness Lee was sent by Watchman Nee and his other co-workers to Taiwan to insure that the things delivered to them by the Lord would not be lost. Watchman Nee instructed Witness Lee to continue the former's publishing operation abroad as the Taiwan Gospel Bookroom, which has been publicly recognized as the publisher of Watchman Nee's works outside China. Witness Lee's work in Taiwan manifested the Lord's abundant blessing. From a mere 350 believers, newly fled from the mainland, the churches in Taiwan grew to 20,000 in five years.

In 1962 Witness Lee felt led of the Lord to come to the United States, settling in California. During his 35 years of service in the U.S., he ministered in weekly meetings and weekend conferences, delivering several thousand spoken messages. Much of his speaking has since been published as over 400 titles. Many of these have been translated into over fourteen languages. He gave his last public conference in February 1997 at the age of 91.

He leaves behind a prolific presentation of the truth in the Bible. His major work, *Life-study of the Bible,* comprises over 25,000 pages of commentary on every book of the Bible from the perspective of the believers' enjoyment and experience of God's divine life in Christ through the Holy Spirit. Witness Lee was the chief editor of a new translation of the New Testament into Chinese called the Recovery Version and directed the translation of the same into English. The Recovery Version also appears in a number of other languages. He provided an extensive body of footnotes, outlines, and spiritual cross references. A radio broadcast of his messages can be heard on Christian radio stations in the United States. In 1965 Witness Lee founded Living Stream Ministry, a non-profit corporation, located in Anaheim, California, which officially presents his and Watchman Nee's ministry.

Witness Lee's ministry emphasizes the experience of Christ as life and the practical oneness of the believers as the Body of Christ. Stressing the importance of attending to both these matters, he led the churches under his care to grow in Christian life and function. He was unbending in his conviction that God's goal is not narrow sectarianism but the Body of Christ. In time, believers began to meet simply as the church in their localities in response to this conviction. In recent years a number of new churches have been raised up in Russia and in many eastern European countries.